A. B. SIMPSON

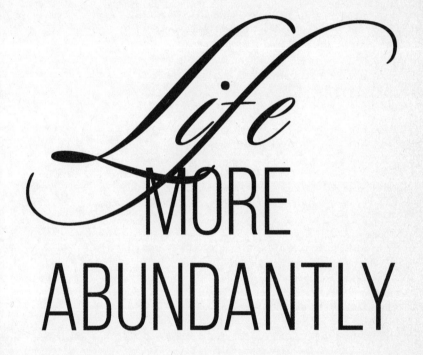

Life MORE ABUNDANTLY

WHITAKER
HOUSE

Unless otherwise indicated, all Scripture quotations are taken from the King James Version of the Holy Bible. Scripture quotations marked (ASV) are taken from the American Standard Edition of the Revised Version of the Holy Bible.

Boldface type in the Scripture quotations indicates the author's emphasis.

LIFE MORE ABUNDANTLY:
A 31-Day Study of God's Greatest Gift

ISBN: 978-1-62911-294-7
eBook ISBN: 978-1-62911-295-4
Printed in the United States of America
© 2015 by Whitaker House

Whitaker House
1030 Hunt Valley Circle
New Kensington, PA 15068
www.whitakerhouse.com

Library of Congress Cataloging-in-Publication Data

Simpson, A. B. (Albert B.)
  Life more abundantly : a 31-day study of God's greatest gift / by A.B. Simpson.
    pages cm
  Includes bibliographical references.
  Summary: "In this monthlong study, famed pastor and evangelist A. B. Simpson delves into the abundant life God promises every believer"— Provided by publisher.
  ISBN 978-1-62911-294-7 (trade pbk. : alk. paper) — ISBN 978-1-62911-295-4 (ebook) 1. Christian life—Meditations. I. Title.
  BV4832.3.S533 2015
  248.4—dc23
                                2014042900

1 2 3 4 5 6 7 8 9 10 11 ⨃ 22 21 20 19 18 17 16 15

CONTENTS

INTRODUCTION

"I am come that they might have life, and that they might have it more abundantly."
—John 10:10

What is life? It is not hard to tell what life does; but what life is, no human definition has yet satisfactorily explained.

The lowest form of organic life in the vegetable kingdom marks the beginning of a new world in nature. The tiny moss on the summit of the mighty mountain, if it could speak and think, might say, "I am greater than this mountain, because I have organic life. The mountain is an inert mass. I spring from a living seed. I grow by a vital process. I drink in nourishment from the air around me and the soil beneath me. I bear my little bud and blossom and leave behind me a living seed that will propagate my kind and give to me through my fruit a perennial life. I live."

The smallest insect on the topmost branches of that magnificent palm tree can look down with just pride on the vegetable kingdom and say, "I am greater than this palm and all the flowers and forests of this land, for I have animal life. I am conscious of my existence, but this palm tree is not. If it were cut down, it would not know it; but I know the joy of living and the pain of suffering. In a still higher sense, I live."

The little child can look up at the mammoth elephant or the noble horse and say, "You could destroy me by the faintest effort; but I am greater than you, for I have intellectual life, I have human life, I have immortal life, I have a life that can be educated until I shall master the elephant and all the strength and cunning of the animal world, and assert my lordship over the whole realm of nature. In a still higher sense, I live."

The most humble and uncultured saint—perhaps a poorest new convert in the jungles of Africa, or a lowly laborer, toiling in some factory or mine—can look in the face of the most brilliant human genius who knows not God in personal faith and fellowship and say, "I live in a higher world than you, for I have spiritual life, I have eternal life, I have a life that death cannot destroy and sin cannot defile and judgment cannot dismay and eternal ages can never end. I have everlasting life."

And yet once more I see a saint of God arise and testify to a yet higher life than all this. "*I am crucified with Christ,*" he cries, "*nevertheless I live*" (Galatians 2:20). And then as even this new life that Christ has given fails to fully satisfy him, I hear him cry yet once more, "*Not I, but Christ liveth in me: and the life which I now live in the flesh I live by the faith of the Son of God, who loved me, and gave himself for me*" (Galatians 2:20). I have not only spiritual life, everlasting life, and the life of the heaven-born soul, but I have divine life, I have the Christ life, I have God Himself to live within me."

Beloved, was this what the Master meant when He said, "*I am come that they might have life, and that they might have it more abundantly*" (John 10:10)? Have you that life, and have you that life more abundantly?

If you were born to perish like the brute, you might be content with the lower forms of life; but as a child of immortality and heir of grace and glory, are you making the most of life?

DAY ONE:

THE TRUE PURPOSE
OF LIFE

"The time is short: it remaineth, that…they that use this
world, [be] as not abusing it."
—1 Corinthians 7:29, 31

What is the supreme significance of life? Is it a pleasant pastime, or is it a solemn probation, a swiftly passing springtime from whose wise sowing the harvests of time and eternity are to be reaped? There is the human side—the beauty, the joy, the romance, the sunshine, and the bloom; but there is the seriousness of life's conflicts—death's tragedy and eternity's mighty issues. No man can make the most of life until he has looked all these things in the face and learned the highest meaning of the old motto *Dum vivimus, vivamus*:

> Live while you live, the epicure would say,
> And seize the pleasures of the present day;
> Live while you live, the sacred preacher cries,
> And give to God each moment as it flies.
> Lord, in my views, let both united be:
> I live in pleasure when I live to thee.[1]

---

1. Philip Doddridge, *Epigram on His Family Arms.*

An old writer compares the worldling to a child sitting on the branches of a fruitful tree, growing over an abyss and thoughtlessly eating the fruit, while two worms, called Day and Night, were slowly eating through the branch, until it suddenly fell and plunged him in the abyss. No man can safely give his supreme attention to earthly things until his eternal interests are insured.

The people that are wasting the springtime of life in thoughtless pleasure may well be compared to the crew of a shipwrecked vessel who were thrown upon a fertile island and succeeded only in saving their cargo of wheat and bringing it ashore. The wise ones suggested that they should plant it in the fertile soil and assure themselves of future supplies, but as they were about to engage in this wise prevision and provision, one of the company returned from an excursion over the hills with the report that he had found a gold mine of inexhaustible wealth. Immediately they all started for the mine and spent the summer in amassing enormous fortunes meanwhile feeding upon the wheat, which they should have planted.

Suddenly, the winds of autumn began to blow, and they awoke with a start to find their food supply well-nigh gone. They eagerly began to plant the remaining seed, but it rotted in the furrows, and they were left to die of starvation, surrounded by millions and billions of worthless gold.

Dear friend, are you wasting life's supreme opportunity like them? Someday, will you hear the blasts of life's autumn moaning over your despairing deathbed *"The harvest is past, the summer is ended, and we are not saved"* (Jeremiah 8:20)? No wise man will go to sleep knowing that the insurance on his property has lapsed without immediately renewing it. And no sane mortal will venture to leave his soul without that divine insurance of which he can say, *"I know whom I have believed, and am persuaded that he is able to keep that which I have committed unto him against that day"* (2 Timothy 1:12).

DAY TWO:

LOSING ONE'S LIFE

"For what shall it profit a man, if he shall gain the whole world, and lose his own soul?"
—Mark 8:36

It is acknowledged by scholars that the word *"soul"* here means "life." But the life of which the Lord was speaking was much more than mere animal existence. The Lord Himself has taught us that *"a man's life consisteth not in the abundance of the things which he possesseth"* and that *"life is more than meat"* (Luke 12:15, 23). Life means all the possibilities of human destiny, both for this life and that which is to come. It is possible to lose one's life in this great and momentous sense. It is possible to miss all the high and glorious things for which existence has been given us, and to be flung aside like a ghastly wreck on the shores of despair, while the wild waves murmur over the pitiful ruin, *"good were it for that man if he had never been born"* (Mark 14:21).

Better that all the ships of all the seas were wrecked, better that some splendid city should sink in an earthquake, better that the world itself should be dissolved in some terrestrial cataclysm, than that one immortal soul should thus be lost. The Word of God is overshadowed with some lurid phrases and figures that hint at such catastrophes. When Jesus spoke of men, He said that they were lost. When He revealed the Father's love in sending His Son,

He did it so that they might not perish. (See John 3:16.) One text ends with the terrible expression "a castaway" (see 1 Corinthians 9:27), and the most loving heart that ever throbbed said of one man that "it were better he had never been born." (See Matthew 26:24.)

The Greek word for *sin* literally means to miss the mark. It is the picture of a lost life, a soul that has missed the way, made a shipwreck of existence, perverted its powers, abused its opportunities, and irretrievably and eternally perished.

But our Master's words suggest that nobody can finally wreck a human soul but man himself. Sin, even the unpardonable sin, is an act of willfulness and recklessness in spite of all the restraint of divine love and grace, and ruined souls shall forever realize that they have lost themselves and been guilty of spiritual and eternal suicide.

The great peril of men and women is that they do not realize the sacredness and solemnity of life. They treat it as a pleasant holiday rather than a great probation and a supreme opportunity. Oh, that God would impress upon every reader of these lines the solemnity of having only one life to live and that life fraught with all the possibilities of endless joy or misery.

> Not many lives, but only one have we,
> One, only one;
> How precious should that one life be—
> That narrow span.

But our text suggests a second question, which sheds the light of hope upon the dark vision of human danger and sin. "*What shall a man give in exchange for his soul?*" (Mark 8:37). If he has lost it, is there any ransom by which it may be recovered?

The Master gave His life to answer that tremendous question. Our life was lost, but we have been redeemed, not with corruptible things, but with the precious blood of Christ. And now He gives us back our lost life and with it His grace to keep that sacred trust from ever again becoming forfeited.

John Newton of England was a wicked sailor who was brought to Christ by an awful dream. One night, as he swung in his hammock on the Adriatic Sea after a day of drunkenness and debauchery, he dreamed that he was standing upon the deck of his ship, holding in his hand a beautiful ring of inestimable value. Suddenly, a demon form appeared before him and dared him to drop it into the sea. Recklessly, he accepted the challenge and flung away his priceless jewel. And the devil danced for joy and told him he had lost his soul, while all along the Adriatic shore, the mountains were lurid with the lightning flames that portended the judgment he had just defied. He was filled with consternation and despair.

Suddenly, the Lord Jesus appeared beside him and asked him if he wished his precious treasure restored. He eagerly begged His help and mercy. The Savior plunged into the wild and stormy sea and at length emerged and reached the deck, holding in His hand the precious jewel, but bearing upon His face the traces of agony and conflict. John Newton threw himself at the Lord's feet and reached out his hand for the precious ring. But the Master held it back and said, "You have thrown away your soul once, and at infinite cost I have redeemed it. I will not again trust it to your keeping but will guard your treasure for you, and it will be awaiting you at the gate of heaven."

The English sailor awoke from his dream to give his life to God and to live for the salvation of his fellow men. So have we been lost and saved. Let us trust Him to keep that which we have committed to His trust.

DAY THREE:

COMING SHORT

*"Let us therefore fear, lest, a promise being left us of entering
into his rest, any of you should seem to come short of it."*
—Hebrews 4:1

To lose one's life utterly and irretrievably is indeed a catastrophe. But to miss the mark and just come short of achieving and attaining is a tragedy of unspeakable pathos.

One of the saddest pictures of the Old Testament is the story of the people that escaped from Egypt, crossed the Jordan, began their march toward the Promised Land, but at the very gates of Canaan, failed to enter in.

They came to the gates of Canaan,
But they never entered in;
They came to the very threshold,
But they perished in their sin.[2]

Two men attempt to leap across a chasm. The one misses the perilous venture by a yard, the other by half an inch; but both are lost. Two men enter a competitive examination on which their future destiny and honor depend. The one completely fails, the other just misses; but the sadder of the two failures is the latter. How solemn is the warning *"Let us therefore fear, lest, a promise*

---

2. Ruth Paxon.

being left us of entering into his rest, any of you should seem to come short of it" (Hebrews 4:1).

Here are two engines. The boilers are both filled with water. In one, the furnace is cold and the fires are out; in the other, the water is hot, the coal is burning, and the temperature is way up above 200 degrees. But both trains are standing still. That boiler must rise to 212 degrees before the piston moves and the train can leave the station. Likewise, it is the fullness of blessing that counts. It is the temperature of the heart that tells. It is the one broken link that makes the whole chain utterly useless and dangerous. It is the last step that counts, and the last half hour that wins.

There is a promise left us of entering into His rest. That promise has been repeated many times and in many forms. It is a promise large and glorious, a promise of victory over sin, Satan, and the world—and of all the possibilities of grace and glory. But its fulfillment is dependent at every step upon our response and our faithfulness. There is a peace that *"passeth all understanding"* (Philippians 4:7), but the condition *"be careful for nothing"* (verse 6) must be met. There is a *"rest"* unto our souls that we may find, but again, the condition is, *"Take my yoke upon you, and learn of me"* (Matthew 11:29). There is a *"great peace"* that *"nothing shall offend"* (Psalm 119:165), but it is given to them that love His law. We may be kept in *"perfect peace"* (Isaiah 26:3), but our mind must be stayed on Him. There is a rest that remaineth for the people of God, but it is only they who believe that enter into rest. Are we meeting these conditions? Are we standing on the ground of faith and taking the place of blessing, or are we coming short?

DAY FOUR:

ETERNAL LIFE

"I give unto them eternal life; and they shall never perish,
neither shall any man pluck them out of my hand."
—John 10:28

We find the Lord Jesus speaking of eternal life. Many persons have an idea that this refers exclusively to our future existence and is a promise of salvation after death. Is this not a narrow and false conception? The life which Christ gives is a kind of life which begins now but belongs to the higher realm of eternal things. There is a striking passage that says, *"He hath set the world in their heart"* (Ecclesiastes 3:11). God lives in eternity, and there is a section of eternity in every human soul. We are too big for this earthly sphere, and have outreachings and needs that belong to the eternal realm. When God saves a man, He puts into him His own life and brings him into touch with a new world of spiritual and eternal realities. *"This is life eternal,"* the Lord Jesus tells us, *"that they might know thee the only true God, and Jesus Christ, whom thou hast sent"* (John 17:3).

Eternal life, therefore, means restoration to the favor and fellowship of God and the creation within us of a new spiritual life, qualified to maintain communion with Him. In a word, it brings us a heaven-born life, that experience which is described technically as "regeneration." We become partakers of the divine nature and the sons of God, not by adoption, but by heavenly birth. This is the special gift of the Lord Jesus to those who receive Him.

> As many as received him, to them gave he power to become the sons of God, even to them that believe on his name: which were born, not of the blood, nor of the will of the flesh, nor of the will of man, but of God. (John 1:12–13)

I was once called to visit a dying boy who had no conception of religion. He had only a few hours to live, and it was a difficult problem to know how to bring conviction to his soul without alarming him. He had no sense of sin and thought he had been so good a boy that he would be all right in the next world. Suddenly, I called the lad's attention to a canary of which he seemed fond, and startled him by asking if they were intimate friends and talked together much about things. The lad was amazed and almost thought I had lost my mind. "Why," he answered, "how could we talk together? He could not understand me; he has only the mind of a bird." Instantly, the application was made.

"Suppose you should find yourself in heaven tomorrow; would you be able to enjoy the companionship of Christ and the saints of God who are there any more than that canary can understand you? You need to have the mind of God put into you, just as much as that bird would need a human mind to understand you."

The simple illustration brought conviction of his need of a new divine life, and, after a little simple teaching and earnest prayer, the light broke, the Lord Jesus came, the life of God touched his dead soul, and, before the next morning had dawned, he had passed triumphantly to the home above. Beloved friend, have you received eternal life, the gift of God through Jesus Christ our Lord?

DAY FIVE:

SPIRITUAL LIFE

"The law of the Spirit of life in Christ Jesus hath made me
free from the law of sin and death."
—Romans 8:2

Two laws are here assumed, the law of sin and death, and the law of the Spirit of life in Christ Jesus. The former bears us down like a fatal and resistless current. The other overcomes that downward trend and lifts us up to righteousness and life. A simple illustration from the natural world will fix these laws vividly in our imagination.

The law of gravitation causes a heavy body to fall to the ground. Under that law, my hand would fall helpless if it were paralyzed and deprived of life. But there is a higher law residing in my will. It is the law of life, and in the exercise of that law, I am able to lift my hand and use it at my will. In like manner, the natural heart is helpless under the law of sin and death, and we are swept into evil by the current of temptation and the impulse of our natural depravity. But the grace of God introduces a new law into the human heart—the law of life, the life of Christ—and through the power of this new principle, we are able to overcome the tendencies of our natural hearts and to will and to do after God's good pleasure. (See Philippians 2:13.)

Apostle Paul vividly portrays the operation of these two laws in the seventh and eighth chapters of Romans. All the force of his own volition, even though he was a regenerated man, was insufficient to overcome the tendency of the old law of sin and death. *"I see another law in my members,"* he cries, *"warring against the law of my mind, and bringing me into captivity to the law of sin which is in my members. O wretched man that I am! who shall deliver me from the body of this death?"* (Romans 7:23–24). It is then that the vision of Christ appears and he exclaims, *"Thank God through Jesus Christ our Lord"* (verse 25). He soon after sums up the philosophy of his supernatural change in the language of our text: *"The law of the Spirit of life in Christ Jesus hath made me free from the law of sin and death"* (Romans 8:2).

Briefly summarized, that law signifies:

1. A new principle of life, a vital force, a spontaneous and automatic impulse that irresistibly overcomes the corruption of our fallen nature and bears the fruits of righteousness just as naturally as the living vine bears its fruit, or as a living man bears himself and his burdens, too.

2. The life of Jesus Christ. This is not a mere human life, not even the new life of the converted soul, but the living Christ Himself united to us and reliving His own life in us.

3. All this is brought about and made real by the Holy Spirit, who comes as the Spirit of life in Christ Jesus, unites us to the Savior, and enables us to live out His life moment by moment. Thus the apostle's testimony is fulfilled: *"I live; yet not I, but Christ liveth in me"* (Galatians 2:20).

Dear friend, are you trying the hopeless experiment of living an ideal Christian life on mere ethical principles? Are you attempting to translate the Sermon on the Mount into your experience by mere force of will and habit? Are you endeavoring to live up to the example of the Lord Jesus Christ by simply putting your feet in His footprints and trying to copy His example? You are doomed to disappointment. Ideals will not do it. Examples will not do it. Ethical principles will not do it. The highest and purest intentions will not do it. It requires a divine Force to live the divine life. The secret was given long ago by the prophet Ezekiel in his message to those to whom he had promised a new heart and a right spirit. But that new heart was not able to overcome the old nature and the forces of evil without a mightier Force behind it, and so he adds, *"I will put my spirit within you, and cause you to walk in my statutes, and ye shall keep my judgments, and do them"* (Ezekiel 36:27). Have you found this causing Power? Have you come into *"the law of the Spirit of life in Christ Jesus"* (Romans 8:2)?

DAY SIX:

SPONTANEOUS LIFE

"I will put my law in their inward parts,
and write it in their hearts."
—Jeremiah 31:33

The highest Christian life is vital, not mechanical. A house is built on mechanical principles by adding section to section from without. A tree is constructed on the vital principle by adding layer upon layer from within. Spiritual life is vital, springing from an inner source and clothing itself with the appropriate expression, manifestation, and fruition. Under the law, men tried to build up a righteousness of effort and external worship and work. It was like the coconuts often seen tied to a palm tree in a heathen graveyard, where the fruit had been attached to the tree as an offering to the spirits of the dead. The fruit was tied on mechanically, and there was a dead man at the root. This is true of all human self-righteousness. Spiritual fruit grows spontaneously from a vital root and a living tree. The Christian does not need so much to try to produce the fruit as to have the life more abundantly. Therefore the Master has said, *"He that abideth in me, and I in him, the same bringeth forth much fruit"* (John 15:5). God is not seeking so much to have us do more for Him as to take more from Him, and thus of His own shall we give back to Him again.

The prophet Jeremiah anticipated this new method of righteousness by his glorious vision of the new covenant which God would make with His people in the New Testament age. He declares, "*I will put my law in their inward parts, and write it in their hearts*" (Jeremiah 31:33). He creates within us a new spontaneous principle of righteousness, which is its own law and manifests itself after its own nature in righteousness, holiness, and love. The principle of Christian obedience is we do it not because we have to but because we love to. This is the automatic force that God uses even in the natural world to accomplish the most extraordinary transformations. What is the explanation of the patient toil of that laboring man who, day after day and year after year, spends his life in his monotonous and grimy task in factory or mine? It is the thought of wife and children, whose loving welcome at night and whose welfare and happiness are his sufficient reward. God holds the world together, with all its countless hearts and homes, by these spontaneous forces of human love. How often have we seen some selfish girl suddenly transformed into a patient, toiling, and happy wife and mother, willing to spend her night in unrequited and extreme labor and sacrifice for her little household, and asking no other recompense than their happiness and affection? So God in the higher realm of grace puts into human hearts the magic secret of a great love, and this transforms selfishness to sacrifice and sordidness to service.

Then there is infinite relief in the delightful positiveness of this higher principle of life. We do not have to be continually thinking of the things we should not do; but keep occupied with Christ, and the light will keep out the darkness and the good will overcome the evil.

The story is told of a river captain who applied for a position at a shipping office in New Orleans. He was asked if he could run a boat on the Mississippi and Ohio. He "reckoned" that he could.

He was then asked if he knew where all the snags were on these dangerous rivers, so that he would be able to avoid them. With a twinkle of his keen eye, he answered, "I reckon I know where the snags ain't, and that is where I expect to do my sailing." It is enough for us to know the channel and hold our course there. It is sufficient to walk on the king's highway and be ignorant of the byways on every side. The true spiritual life is a very simple matter, and there is infinite comfort and sufficient help for the wayfaring man though a fool to walk therein. Have we learned the secret and, step by step and day by day, are we living it out according to His own simple word, *"As ye have therefore received Christ Jesus the Lord, so walk ye in him"* (Colossians 2:6)?

> Tis so sweet to walk with Jesus,
> Step by step and day by day;
> Stepping in His very footprints,
> Walking with Him all the way.[3]

---

3. A. B. Simpson, "Step by Step," 1897.

DAY SEVEN:

THE CHRIST LIFE

"I live; yet not I, but Christ liveth in me."
—Galatians 2:20

The dream of ancient mythology and art was to bring the gods down into fellowship with men. They succeeded only in degrading their ideals of deity by the weakness of human passion. The gospel alone has given this stupendous revelation and transformation. Two mysteries are involved. The first is the incarnation of God in the human life of the Lord Jesus Christ. And the second is the incarnation of Christ in the human life of a consecrated Christian. Apostle Paul has expressed this double mystery in a fine passage in Colossians. It reads, *"In him dwelleth all the fulness of the Godhead bodily. And ye are complete in him"* (Colossians 2:9–10). This might be paraphrased with perfect truthfulness—God fills Jesus Christ, and Jesus Christ fills me. The word *"complete"* in this passage literally means to "fill full."

This doctrine of the indwelling Christ is peculiarly Pauline. The Lord Jesus had anticipated it in the gospel of John when He spoke of the branches and the vine and summed up our spiritual life in the striking words *"Abide in me, and I in you.…For without me ye can do nothing"* (John 15:4–5). But it was reserved especially for Paul, above all the later writers of the New Testament, to realize and reveal this glorious mystery. It was the secret of his own life. The first chapter of that marvelous life is described by him in these words: *"It pleased God…to reveal his Son in me"* (Galatians 1:15–16). From that time, he lived a charmed life, he was possessed and controlled by a power that transcended all his mere human possibilities of character and action. It was another life, an added life, an overmastering and all sufficient life, *"the life also of Jesus"* (2 Corinthians 4:10). He was enabled to overcome sin and temptation and to live out His Christian life and accomplish his marvelous work not through his own personal capabilities merely but through a union with the Lord Jesus—a union so intimate and complete that all the strength and purity and love of the Master's being absolutely possessed him and so identified him with Christ that what Christ thought and felt and did, he also thought and felt and did, and he could literally say, *"I live; yet not I, but Christ liveth in me"* (Galatians 2:20).

This became to him the passionate ambition of his ministry, the great open secret that he had been commissioned to make known to all the world. He speaks of it in the first chapter of Colossians as the secret that had been hidden from ages and generations but was now made known to him and committed to him to make known to all men. That secret he declares is *"Christ in you, the hope of glory"* (Colossians 1:27).

The Christ life! Can we realize all that it means! It stands at once for the highest level of holy aspiration and the lowest reach of divine grace. It offers us something infinitely higher than mere human perfection, for it is nothing less than the holiness of God divinely imparted to us through the Lord Jesus Christ. But at the same time, it is not an attainment slowly achieved by long and patient endeavor. It is not a mountaintop scaled by the weary feet of human effort. It is a great obtainment, a divine gift, a life brought down to us by the living One Himself and offered to the most helpless struggling soul through the infinite condescension and grace of the Lord Jesus Christ, so that each of us can say, no matter how often we have failed or how helpless we may feel, "wondrous grace, it reaches me."[4]

And finally, it is maintained not from our strength or steadfastness but through simply abiding in Him and moment by moment realizing *"of his fulness have all we received, and grace for grace"* (John 1:16).

---

4. Mary D. James, "It Reaches Me."

DAY EIGHT:

CHRIST FOR THE MIND

"We have the mind of Christ."
—1 Corinthians 2:16

We have been so long accustomed to limit the operation of the Christian religion to what we call the "spiritual realm" that we overlook the provision of the gospel for the quickening of our intellectual life. The apostle prays that the whole spirit and soul and body of the Thessalonians be preserved blameless unto the coming of the Lord. The soul evidently represents our intellectual nature. This has its place in the divine scheme of entire sanctification. In another place, the apostle speaks of the power of grace *"casting down imaginations…and bringing into captivity every thought to the obedience of Christ"* (2 Corinthians 10:5).

In our text, we are said to have the mind of Christ. This is the climax of a long argument in the course of which the writer has been aiming to show that the mere psychical faculties of the human understanding are insufficient to apprehend spiritual truth and that we need a divine and spiritual touch in our understanding to enable us to *"know the things that are freely given to us of God"* (1 Corinthians 2:12). This he finally expresses by the striking phrase *"we have the mind of Christ."*

The Lord Jesus Christ in His incarnate life was a perfect Man with a "true body" and "a reasonable soul"; and if His inner life was normal, it involved the possession of a spiritual nature and a soul or mind. Now, if Christ is our living Head and imparts to us His complete life, it is reasonable to assume that He becomes to us the Source not only of spiritual but of intellectual life and imparts His quickening life to our mind as well as to our spirit.

What a vast world of possibilities this opens to our faith! In the first place, it means, of course, the cleansing of our mind from all sinful thoughts, false conceptions of truth, unholy affections, and forbidden occupations or recreations. The mind of Christ will not waste its powers on worldly amusements or worthless and frivolous reading.

But it means much more than this negative side. It means the filling of the consecrated mind with the thoughts of God, the affections that are above, and the occupations that uplift us and bless others. Certainly it involves the quickening, stimulating, and strengthening of all our mental powers and a divine addition to all the forces and resources of our intellectual life. The gifts of the Holy Spirit include divine wisdom, knowledge, and a quickened memory.

In the Old Testament, we are told of the men that designed and built the Hebrew tabernacle having been divinely anointed with special gifts of wisdom required for the cunning workmanship and the expert construction of that simple but magnificent work of art. The women of Israel received the same enduement for their exquisite embroidery employed in the decoration of the sanctuary. David ascribes his military skill and strength to divine enabling. The apostles were supernaturally quickened for their marvelous grasp of truth and their power of forceful expression. While the grace of God will not supersede all proper human effort and culture and offers no premium to indolence, yet when all our powers are wholly dedicated to the service of Christ, we may surely expect an infinite, divine addition to our mere human capabilities. How often have we seen some converted drunkard, whose physical powers and mental faculties had been practically destroyed by a life of dissipation, not only transformed spiritually, but mentally quickened and seemingly inspired with a supernatural grasp of truth and power of expression, and used by God in unspeakable blessing for the uplifting of his fellow men. This is nothing less than the mind of Christ. Have we fully realized all the possibilities of our intellectual life under the leading and teaching of the Holy Spirit?

The quickening of the memory is distinctly referred to in the promise of the Comforter. *"He shall…bring all things to your remembrance, whatsoever I have said unto you"* (John 14:26).

Perhaps the most prolific source of our worries and troubles is found in our mental sphere. The regulation of our thoughts is the special work of the Holy Spirit. He is able to bring every thought into captivity to the obedience of Christ. The peace of God, which passes all understanding not only keeps the heart but keeps the mind. (See Philippians 4:7.) Under His gracious control, how…

Every doubt and fear would vanish,
Every doubt and conflict cease,
Love would sway a boundless empire
O'er a realm of perfect peace.

DAY NINE:

A HIGHER PHYSICAL LIFE

*"The life also of Jesus might be made manifest
in our mortal flesh."*
—2 Corinthians 4:11

The medical science and the medical congresses of our day are much concerned about the physical improvement of the race, and some of their theories are radical and astounding. Eugenics has become a science, and the propagation of a perfect race a study for the wisdom of the world, and it is even proposed that national legislation shall so control the propagation of the species, that all the imperfect product shall be rendered impossible and the highest types of humanity alone be permitted to survive.

In all this, the wisdom of the world, which is foolishness with God (see 1 Corinthians 3:19), has constantly lost sight of God's supernatural provision for the quickening and conserving of our physical life and strength. As long ago as the age of Moses, God revealed to man a divine law of healing and manifested Himself by a new name: *"I am the LORD that healeth thee [Jehovah Rophi]"* (Exodus 15:26). In the darkest period of Hebrew history, He gave to the world in the story of Samson the divine secret of physical strength—the Holy Spirit in a separated and consecrated body. Flashes of this truth again and again appear throughout the Old Testament in the psalms of David, the story of Hezekiah, and the prophecies of Isaiah and Malachi. But at length, the Lord Jesus Christ appeared as the Great Physician and not only ministered life and healing to the bodies of men but left a law of healing for His church to the end of time. This divine secret of physical life is again and again unfolded in the New Testament epistles, and it may be summed up in a few simple principles:

1. It is founded upon the atonement of Christ for spirit, soul, and body.

2. It is claimed through the name of Jesus by virtue of His merits.

3. It is by faith, not works, a direct act of God Himself rather than the result of human skill and effort. (See Ephesians 2:8–9.)

4. It requires that the subject of it should be rightly adjusted to the will of God, separated from known sin and wholly yielded and consecrated to the will and service of the Lord.

5. It is imparted by the Holy Spirit. *"If the Spirit of him that raised up Jesus from the dead dwell in you, he that raised up Christ from the dead shall also quicken your mortal bodies by his Spirit that dwelleth in you"* (Romans 8:11).

6. The essence and nature of the life that the Spirit brings into our physical being is nothing less than the life of Jesus Christ Himself. Not only did He have on earth a human body like us, but He has that body still. The resurrection of Christ was physical, and His present heavenly body is as perfect and capable of imparting life and strength to us as His glorified Spirit. *"We are members of his body"* (Ephesians 5:30), and the apostle teaches us in our text that even when our own physical powers seem to be exhausted, *"the life also of Jesus"* (2 Corinthians 4:11) may be manifest in our mortal flesh.

7. This supernatural life of Christ is not merely imparted through an occasional act of miraculous power but maintained by the habit of abiding fellowship with Him and dependence on Him. He Himself has said, *"As the living Father hath sent me, and I live by the Father: so he that eateth me, even he shall live by me"* (John 6:57). And again, in the chapter from which our text is taken, the apostle declares, *"Though our outward man perish, yet the inward man is renewed day by day"* (2 Corinthians 4:16).

In his third epistle, the apostle John prays for his well-beloved friend a most significant petition. He says, *"I wish above all things that thou mayest prosper and be in health, even as thy soul prospereth"* (3 John 1:2). What an ideal of physical soundness and strength keeping pace with spiritual healthfulness! Surely this is in the highest sense "a sound mind in a sound body."

Beloved reader, are you living up to this high ideal? Are you having God's best for your entire being—spirit, soul, and body?

DAY TEN:

THE SPIRIT-FILLED LIFE

"Be filled with the Spirit."
—Ephesians 5:18

The epistle to the Ephesians is the epistle of the Spirit. Its opening ascription is a doxology to God *"who hath blessed us with all the spiritual blessings in heavenly places in Christ"* (Ephesians 1:3).

After giving us in the first chapter and the thirteenth verse a reference to the sealing of the Holy Spirit as the initial act of a consecrated life, he goes on to expand the fullness of the Spirit through the succeeding chapters in a number of striking passages. At length in the fifth chapter, he sums it all up in the injunction *"Be filled,"* or *"[Being] filled with the Spirit."* We are, therefore, reminded that the resources of the Holy Spirit are large and boundless, and we must not for a moment conclude because of any blessing that we have already received that we have exhausted them.

What is it to be filled with the Spirit?

1. Surely, it means to have all the operations, graces, and gifts of the Spirit. That is, to have Him in all His fullness. He is the Spirit of light; has He enlightened our darkness and become our spiritual vision, sight as well as light? He is the Spirit of Life; has He quickened our dead nature in regeneration and given us His life more abundantly?

He is the Spirit of holiness; has He cleansed our hearts
and imparted to us the holiness of Christ? He is the
Spirit of truth; is He leading us into all truth? He is the
Spirit of love; has He set our hearts on fire and translated
1 Corinthians 13 into our life? He is the Spirit of peace
and joy; has He given us the *"peace of God, which passeth
all understanding"* (Philippians 4:7), and the fullness of
His joy? He is the Spirit of prayer; has He not only taught
us to pray for ourselves but led us into the life of prayer
and the ministry of prayer for others? He is the Spirit of
power; has He endued us with divine energy and made us
witnesses unto Christ to our fellow men in saving power?
In a word, have we received the Holy Spirit in all the variety of His gifts and ministries?

2.   It means that not only should we have all there is of Him
but He should have all there is of us. Is every part of our
being filled with the Spirit? Have we received Him into
our spiritual nature to lift us up into the life of God? Have
we received Him into our intellectual nature to cleanse,
to quicken, and to use it? Have we received Him into our
physical being to purify every member, to consecrate every
power, to heal and to employ our lips and hands and feet
and all our ransomed powers for the service and glory of
Christ? This is what it means to be filled with the Spirit.

3.   And it means to be filled with Him in all the circumstances, seasons, moments, interests, and occupations of
our life. It means the immanence of God in all our human
relationships and activities. It means to have Him in our
business, in our trials, in our joys, in our gains and losses,
in our family affairs, in the whole circumference of life. It
is the spiritual application of the miracle of the widow's

oil poured out into all the vessels of our diversified human life.

There's no time too busy for His leisure;
There's no task too hard for Him to bear;
There's no soul too lowly for His notice;
There's no need too trifling for His care;
There's no place too lonely for His presence;
There's no pain His bosom cannot feel;
There's no sorrow that He cannot comfort;
There's no sickness that He cannot heal.

Have we been thus filled with the Spirit? Better yet, are we being thus continually refilled with the Holy Spirit? Are we living in the atmosphere of His presence? Is His life the very element of our being? "Be *being filled* with the Spirit."

DAY ELEVEN:

RESURRECTION LIFE

*"That I may know him, and the power of his resurrection,
and the fellowship of his sufferings, being made conformable
unto his death; if by any means I might attain unto the
resurrection of the dead."*
—Philippians 3:10–11

The profoundest principle of the Christian religion is death and resurrection. It is foreshadowed in some of the most important processes of nature—the planting and germinating of the seed, the succession of winter and spring, the alternation of day and night, the beautiful parable of the chrysalis and the butterfly. All these are types of the sacred mystery of the cross and the resurrection of our Lord and Savior Jesus Christ. The symbolic rites and types of the old dispensation, the flood, the crossing of the Red Sea and the Jordan, the rite of circumcision, the eighth day initiating a new week—all these pointed forward to the new creation and found at last their highest fulfillment in the cross and the open tomb.

The testimony of the New Testament witnesses always centered in the resurrection. *"This Jesus hath God raised up, whereof we all are witnesses"* (Acts 2:32). But the resurrection is not an isolated and stupendous fact relating alone to the Lord Jesus, the Firstborn from the dead, but is repeated and realized in the personal experience of each of His followers. While this is yet to become gloriously real in the literal resurrection of the bodies of the saints, it has a deeply spiritual application in the history of every true believer. *"I am crucified with Christ: nevertheless I live"* (Galatians 2:20) is the most distinctive watchword of the divine life. Practical Christianity is not an ethical reformation; it is a divine creation and a new creation. It is a death born life.

But the practical bearing of this great mystery depends to a great extent upon the measure and degree in which we fully apprehend, realize, and enter into it. This is the significance of the apostle's prayer *"That I may know…the power of his resurrection"* (Philippians 3:10).

In the first place, the resurrection of Christ sets us free from guilt and seals our justification. The Pauline theory of salvation is that the man who sinned has been crucified with Christ and is reckoned dead, and that the real man, whom God recognizes and whom we should recognize in ourselves, is the life that was born out of Christ—the new life, the risen life, the life that is as free from liability for our past sins as Christ Himself. *"He that is dead is freed from sin"* (Romans 6:7).

But it means much more than this. Positively it brings us into actual identification with the vital and omnipotent potency of the life of the Lord Jesus. Our spiritual life is not the struggle of an earnest will and an upright spirit against the power of evil; it is the all sufficient strength of the Lord Jesus Himself living in us and overcoming the forces of evil, so that we think and feel and act as Christ would through the power of the Christ that lives within us.

But not only so, it means a supernatural vision and a practical realization of our complete fellowship with our risen Lord in all that His resurrection meant. The apostle Paul gives us an unveiling of this vision in Ephesians 1:18–21. It is a dazzling vision of mountain piled upon mountain, and height transcending height, revealing all…

> *...the riches of the glory of his inheritance in the saints, and what is the exceeding greatness of his power to us-ward who believe, according to the working of his mighty power, which he wrought in Christ, when he raised him from the dead, and set him at his own right hand in the heavenly places, far above all principality, and power, and might, and dominion, and every name that is named, not only in this world, but also in that which is to come.*

All this has been achieved by Him; and in all this, He is our Head and Forerunner, and we are authorized to claim the *"power of his resurrection"* (Philippians 3:10) and the fellowship of His risen and ascension life. This was the intense outreaching to which Paul tries to give expression in the magnificent chapter from which our text is taken. For this he has been apprehended of Christ and is pressing out to meet that divine attraction, that upward calling which is seeking to apprehend him. It is through this that he is enabled to stoop to the lower depths of the *"fellowship of his sufferings"* (verse 10); and it is by virtue of this that He expects at last to rise to the final attainment of all that is meant by the *"resurrection of the dead"* (verse 11) at the glorious appearing of the Lord.

DAY TWELVE:

TRANSFIGURED LIVES

*"Be not conformed to this world: but be ye transformed by
the renewing of your mind, that ye may prove what is that
good, and acceptable, and perfect, will of God."*
—Romans 12:2

The transfiguration of Christ not only made His face to shine
as the sun but His raiment also to be *"white as the light"* (Matthew
17:2). Mark tells us that His raiment became shining, *"exceeding
white as snow; so as no fuller on earth can white them"* (Mark 9:3).
Luke tells us *"his raiment was white and glistering"* (Luke 9:29).

Now this raiment was nothing more than the coarse and ordinary tunic that he wore in his daily life and that was woven of
ordinary materials and perhaps much worn and threadbare. And
yet in the transfiguration light, that common texture became more
glorious than burnished metal or resplendent gold.

Now this is just what a transfigured life means. It is not something transcendental or unearthly but an ordinary, everyday life
touched by the grace of God and the glory of heaven, and shining
as a little bit of broken glass sometimes shines with jeweled bright-
ness under the rays of the sun.

The twelfth chapter of Romans is a picture of a homely, practical, everyday life. It takes us into the church, of course, and reminds

us of our oneness with our brethren and of our various gifts and ministries, and it bids us to be faithful whether in teaching, giving, administering executive departments of work, dispensing charity to the poor, or exhorting saints and sinners. Then it introduces us to the home and social circle and talks about love without dissimulation, kindly affection, mutual consideration, hospitality, condescension to men of low estate, adjustment to all kinds of people, sympathetic joy with those that are happy, sympathetic tears with those that weep, and all those beautiful graces and amenities of life that count so largely in a happy home and a perfect character.

Next, it accompanies us to the street, the store, and the business circle; and it makes us diligent, capable, "[providing] *things honest in the sight of all men*" (Romans 12:17), "*not slothful in business*" (Romans 12:11), and yet at the same time devout in the midst of secular surroundings, still "*serving the Lord*" (verse 11).

Then it finds a place not only for the noonday prayer meeting and the morning and evening altar but for the life of prayer, for the atmosphere of devotion, for a spirit that is ever attuned to heavenly things, and in communion with our heavenly Father, for we read in the very heart of this picture, "*Continuing instant in prayer*" (Romans 12:12).

Nor does it give a one-sided picture of easy conditions and a life wholly free from trial, temptation, and even persecution and wrong. For again we read, "*Bless them which persecute you*" (Romans 12:14); "*Recompense to no man evil for evil*" (verse 17); "*If it be possible...live peaceably with all men*" (verse 18); "*Avenge not yourselves*" (verse 19); "*If thine enemy hunger, feed him; if he thirst, give him drink*" (verse 20). Surely, this is a life environed with trial and suffering, and yet all these conditions are recognized as opportunities for victory and transfiguration. It needs the night to bring out the glory of the stars. It requires the storm cloud to make it possible to paint the rainbow. And so,

> Sorrow, touched by Thee, grows bright,
> With more than rapture's ray.[5]

Beloved, this is a transfigured life—a man walking with his feet on earth but his head and heart amid the glory of the skies; a life occupied with earthly things, but in a heavenly spirit and a spiritual way; a life made up of days divided, as Sir William Jones used to divide his day of twenty-four hours: "Eight for labor, eight for recreation and food, eight for sleep—but all for heaven."

The glory that transfigures such a life comes from above and from within. We are transfigured by the renewing of our mind. It is the temple of glass devoted to the sun in the worship of ancient Egypt, in which the sun has free access to every chamber and sheds his own glory in every part.

Finally, there is a suggestion of the highest possibilities of such a life in the positive, comparative, and superlative degrees of our beautiful text, the *"good, and acceptable,"* and, higher and better, the *"perfect...will of God"* (Romans 12:2).

---

5. Thomas Moore, "O Thou Who Driest the Mourner's Tear," 1816.

DAY THIRTEEN:

RADIANT LIVES

"They looked unto him, and were lightened."
—Psalm 34:5

The most remarkable discovery of recent scientific research is radium. The most remarkable thing about it is that it radiates or gives forth its light and power with almost inexhaustible energy. A few grains would be sufficient to explode the planet. A small quantity, and there is but a small quantity in the world, would be equivalent to a million and a half tons of coal and would contain sufficient energy to carry an Atlantic steamer on her regular voyages to and fro for a whole generation. It would take more than seventeen centuries for a grain of radium to exhaust itself by radiation. One flash of radial light would go round the globe in less than a second.

And yet this remarkable element comes from the dark mine where it has been trodden underfoot of men and is scarcely distinguishable from common tar. It is found in a substance called pitch blend, strongly resembling tar. How it speaks to us of these lives of ours lifted from obscurity, despair, and from the depths of sin, and destined through the grace of God to shine as the stars forever and ever.

And how it inspires us, like radium, to *"let* [our] *light so shine before men, that they may see your good works, and glorify your Father which is in heaven"* (Matthew 5:16).

We are told that radium has six different colored rays differentiated in the solar spectrum and numbered a, b, c, d, e, and f in the scientific catalogs.

The first radiant ray that should be reflected from our lives is the light of truth. God calls us to be living epistles, known and read of all men, and the writing should be a living edition of His own Word. Someone has said that we are either Bibles or libels. Are our lives revealing Christ and His gospel to our fellow men and, as the apostle strongly puts it, *"adorn[ing] the doctrine of God our Saviour in all things"* (Titus 2:10)?

The next manifestation of our light should be purity. The greatest thing in every true life is a holy personal character. The greatest thing the Lord Jesus did was not to teach but to be the truth and the life. His moral victory over the tempter in the wilderness made it possible for Him to become our Righteousness. Are we living the Christ we profess and the truth we confess?

But our lives ought not only to be right but attractive. God wants us to show the light of loveliness, the charm of Jesus, the things that are lovely as well as the things that are pure. Many Christians are like a naked cliff, strong and upright but bare and unattractive. The true ideal is the mountain adorned with verdure and flowers and fountains where the traveler rests and the children play. The Lord Jesus even in His earliest childhood had favor with God and men. The epistle to the Philippians is a beautiful picture of the beauty of holiness. Without it, we cannot be God's best.

The light of patience is the crowning glory of the saint. It is through patience that grace has its perfect work and leaves the soul perfect and entire, wanting nothing.

This is the light that shines in darkness and irradiates the home of sorrow, the house of mourning, and the valley of the shadow of death. Let your light so shine.

The light of love is the most precious of all the radiant beams of holy character. It makes the homeliest face attractive and the humblest home a paradise. It can overcome evil with good, transform the curse into a blessing, and conquer all our enemies by killing them with kindness. Are we letting the light of love shine on the little world around us, the dark world beneath us, and the lost world beyond us?

> As the sunshine, free and glad,
> Falls where gloom and squalor pine;
> So where all is dark and sad,
> On the good and on the bad,
> Let your light so shine.

DAY FOURTEEN:

THE VICTORIOUS LIFE

"Thanks be unto God,
which always causeth us to triumph in Christ."
—2 Corinthians 2:14

Have we fully realized the sublime ideal here presented—
"always...to triumph"? Is it indeed possible that in this life of infirmity, temptation, and unfavorable environment, the soldier of the Lord may always overcome?

The answer will not be so hard if we continually keep before our mind the closing words of our text: *"in Christ."* It is in Christ and in Christ alone that we may always triumph.

Another reading of the passage throws a strong light upon it:
"Thanks be unto God, who always leadeth us in triumph in Christ"
(2 Corinthians 2:14 ASV). He is the Leader, the Victor, and the Captain of our salvation, and we simply enter into His triumph.

This thought becomes intensely practical. Are we pressed by the conflict with sin? Are we fighting hard against the evil that insinuates itself from within and seems to be part of our own nature and disposition? Mere resistance, however sincere and strenuous, will not suffice. There is a better way. Christ has already conquered sin, and it is our privilege to enter into His victory. We have a right to claim that by our union with Him, we are dead indeed unto sin and its authority and power are broken, and also that we are risen with Him to vital fellowship in His new and victorious life. As we thus identify ourselves with Him, we are able through His indwelling life and power to throw off the old man and his deeds, to recognize all evil as extraneous to us, neither fearing it nor obeying it, and to appropriate His holiness, His love, His power, and His all-sufficiency, going forth with the triumphant shout *"Thanks be unto God, which always causeth us to triumph in Christ"* (2 Corinthians 2:14).

Is it sorrow that overwhelms us from without and within until our spirit is ready to sink in utter depression and discouragement? Here again the ethics of human philosophy fail and the most stoical indifference and fortitude must at last succumb. But again, it is our privilege to triumph in Christ. He has overcome the world; He was victorious over sorrow and every circumstance and condition; and it is our privilege to enter into His joy and draw from Him a consolation wholly apart from conditions and surroundings and which is nothing less than His own joy filling and overflowing our heart. *"These things have I spoken unto you, that my joy might remain in you, and that your joy might be full"* (John 15:11). There is a peace that *"passeth all understanding"* (Philippians 4:7), that is, has no rational explanation and contradicts all seeming conditions. There is a joy that *"count[s] it all joy"* (James 1:2) when it feels no joy and sees no light. There is a faith which can glory even in tribulation and rise from the deepest abysses of trouble to the sublimest heights of victory and praise. The life of faith is a continual paradox expressed in such terms as these: *"When I am weak, then am I strong"* (2 Corinthians 12:10); *"Sorrowful, yet alway rejoicing;… having nothing, and yet possessing all things"* (2 Corinthians 6:10).

Perhaps our greatest conflict is with the forces of temptation. People who deny the existence of the devil would soon be convinced if they really made an honest resistance to his power. But our text gives us the secret of victory over Satan. It is not our victory but Christ's. He is a reckless Man who defies the devil or attempts to meet him in his own strength. But when we meet him in Christ, he is already a conquered foe, and it is our privilege to enter into the victory of the Lord and meet all our temptations with the prestige of assured triumph and a shout of victory—*"Thanks be unto God, which always causeth us to triumph in Christ"* (2 Corinthians 2:14).

DAY FIFTEEN:

MORE THAN CONQUERORS

"In all these things we are more than conquerors
through him that loved us."
—Romans 8:37

We have spoken of victory, but this is more than victory. This is a triumph so complete that we have not only escaped defeat and destruction but we have destroyed our enemies and won a spoil so rich and valuable that we can thank God that the battle ever came.

How can we be *"more than conquerors"* (Romans 8:37)?

In the first place, we can get out of the conflict a spiritual discipline that will greatly strengthen our faith and establish our spiritual character. Temptation is necessary to settle and confirm us in the spiritual life. It is like the fire that burns in the colors of a mineral painting, or like winds that cause the mighty cedars of the mountain to strike their roots more deeply into the soil. Our spiritual conflicts are among our choicest blessings, and our great adversary is used to train us for his own ultimate defeat.

Again, temptation is permitted to come to us to give us the opportunity of weakening and destroying our spiritual adversaries. There is a remarkable statement in the book of Joshua about the Canaanites. *"It was of the* Lord*...that they should come against*

Israel…that he might destroy them" (Joshua 11:20). Had they remained neutral or passive, they might later have become a snare, but their defiance led to their destruction and saved the hosts of Joshua from later perils and conflicts. So God allows things that are lurking in our nature to assert themselves in order to reveal to us these hidden sources of danger and bring to an issue a conflict that deepens our own spiritual life and leads to the uprooting and destroying of hidden sin. Thus God will bring to light, as we are to bear it, all the things in our spiritual life that need to be discovered and destroyed, and we shall learn to thank Him for each new conflict because it assures a deeper life and a more complete deliverance from all the power of evil.

Temptation brings us a glorious confirmation of our confidence in God and proves the reality of His promises and the faithfulness of His love and grace. Each new triumph reassures us for all the conflicts that are to come, and we learn to realize that we are following a Captain that never knew defeat and that it is indeed possible to always triumph in Christ Jesus.

The ancient Phrygians had a legend that every time they conquered an enemy, the victor absorbed the physical strength of his victim and added so much more to his own strength and valor. So temptation victoriously met doubles our spiritual strength and equipment. It is possible thus not only to defeat our enemy but to capture him and make him fight in our own ranks.

The prophet Isaiah speaks of flying on the shoulders of the Philistines. These Philistines were their deadly foes, but the figure suggested that they would be enabled not only to conquer the Philistines but to use them to carry the victors on their shoulders for further triumphs. Just as the wise sailor can use a headwind to carry him forward by tacking and taking advantage of its impelling force, so it is possible for us in our spiritual life, through the victorious grace of God, to turn to account the things that seem most unfriendly and unfavorable and to be able continually to say, *"The things which happened unto me have fallen out rather unto the furtherance of the gospel"* (Philippians 1:12).

Finally, the conflict will bring us the victor's crown and the glorious promise *"To him that overcometh"* (Revelation 3:21). Shall we be *"more than conquerors"*?

DAY SIXTEEN:

GETTING THE BEST OF TROUBLE

"That the trial of your faith, being much more precious than of gold which perisheth, though it be tried with fire, might be found unto praise and honour and glory at the appearing of Jesus Christ."
—1 Peter 1:7

The first epistle of Peter is a special message for the tried ones and shows us how we may be *"more than conquerors"* over sorrow.

The apostle tells us some very comforting things about our trials. They are *"for a season"* (1 Peter 1:6), he tells us. There is a *"need be"* (verse 6), which we shall some time understand. The trial itself is *"much more precious than of gold that perisheth"* (verse 7). And it will *"be found unto praise and honour and glory at the appearing of Jesus Christ"* (verse 7).

These three words are not repetitions. *"Praise"* expresses the thankfulness with which we ourselves will look back on all the things that once seemed so hard and praise Him for the inexorable love that let us suffer to gain such blessing. The *"honour"* refers to the bearing of our victorious suffering on the glory of God. It reflects honor on Christ. And the word *"glory"* looks forward to the recompense when our *"light affliction, which is but for a moment"* will have worked out for us yonder "*a far more exceeding and eternal weight of glory*" (2 Corinthians 4:17). The only way we can win the crown is by suffering and sacrifice. Someday, our teardrops will be transformed to jewels of unfading luster.

Later in the epistle, he adds some further considerations to encourage us in this suffering life. He tells us that when we suffer wrongfully, it is "*thankworthy*" (1 Peter 2:19) and "*acceptable with God*" (verse 20). The phrase is peculiar, suggesting the idea that God Himself will express to us His own special thanks for the service that we have rendered Him in thus witnessing for Him. The phrase is twice repeated. What an honor it will be someday for the King to step from the throne and publicly thank us for what we once endured for Him!

Then in the twenty-first verse of the same chapter, we are reminded that this is our calling: "*Hereunto were ye called: because Christ also suffered for us, leaving us an example, that* [we] *should follow his steps*" (1 Peter 2:21). Trial is our business, suffering our occupation. Suppose a soldier were to complain to his captain that the enemy had been firing on him and that he did not enlist for any such purpose and was unwilling to submit to that kind of treatment. We can imagine his commander saying, "My boy, the business of a soldier is to be fired at." Shall we cease to complain about the wrongs of men or murmur against the chastening of our Father and say, "*The cup which my Father hath given me, shall I not drink it?*" (John 18:11).

Finally, the supreme encouragement to victorious suffering is that it means partnership with Christ. "*Rejoice, inasmuch as ye are partakers of Christ's sufferings; that, when his glory shall be revealed, ye may be glad also with exceeding joy*" (1 Peter 4:13). Every loyal Christian heart must long to be like unto Him in all things. Thank God the fellowship is double. "*If we suffer* [with Him], *we shall also reign with him*" (2 Timothy 2:12); if we share the cross, we shall wear the crown.

DAY SEVENTEEN:

GETTING THE BEST OF MISFORTUNE

"And his mother called his name Jabez, saying,
Because I bare him with sorrow....And God granted
him that which he requested."
—1 Chronicles 4:9–10

This is the pathetic picture of a life which in its beginning at least was typical of many an earthly story. "Little Misery" we might appropriately call this child of misfortune who came into the world under a cloud of pessimism. His very mother refused to welcome him. Perhaps there were conditions in her pregnancy that made his advent only a suggestion of shame and sorrow. His childhood was overshadowed with gloom, perhaps neglect and every discouragement. At last there was nothing left for him but God, and we read that *"Jabez called on the God of Israel, saying, Oh that thou wouldest bless me indeed, and enlarge my coast, and that thine hand might be with me, and that thou wouldest keep me from evil, that it may not grieve me!"* (1 Chronicles 4:10). And the next sentence is a glorious burst of sunshine that obliterates all his clouds and makes the life of Jabez a romance of answered prayer and sorrow transformed to blessing. *"And God granted him that which he requested"* (verse 10).

Yes, it is possible to be *"more than conquerors"* over the most adverse circumstances and the most forbidding beginnings. The Valley of Achor has often become a Door of Hope and the thorn been changed to the myrtle and the fir tree. The secret of it all is the touch of God in answer to the prayer of emergency and faith.

Jabez's prayer began in the right place. *"Oh that thou wouldest bless me indeed."* He did not ask first that circumstances might be changed but that he might be changed and adjusted to God and circumstances. If there is anything the matter with our lives, it is usually true that most of the matter is with ourselves. A heart right with God and filled with the life and joy of Christ could not be unhappy even in the depths of hell. Let us, therefore, first begin at home.

Then Jabez caught a larger vision and prayed that God would enlarge his coast. (See 1 Corinthians 4:10.) His surroundings were uncongenial, but there was room further on, and he asked God to give him a bigger world. The reason many people are so unhappy is because they live in so small a circle. Get out of your little sphere of selfishness and into the great world where God dwells and where other hearts touch you and call you to help their sorrows, and you can have as big a heritage as you will make.

Next Jabez said, *"That thine hand might be with me"* (1 Corinthians 4:10). He wanted a life with God, divinely led, divinely sufficient. With such an equipment, what could be against him?

Then his last petition is finely significant: *"Keep me from evil, that it may not grieve me!"* (verse 10). He did not ask that there might be no clouds in his sky or thorns in his path, but that he might be impervious to their sting and proof against their power to harm. God's grace can take the evil out of everything so that sorrow will lose its bitterness, hate its power to harm us, and death its sting.

Then shall we look at the hard places in our lives not as discouragements but as challenges, things that God has permitted, that He may overcome them and that we may be lifted through the conflict to a higher place of victorious strength and blessing.

DAY EIGHTEEN:

GETTING THE BEST OF CIRCUMSTANCES

"I have learned, in whatsoever state I am, therewith to be content. I know both how to be abased, and I know how to abound: every where and in all things I am instructed both to be full and to be hungry, both to abound and to suffer need. I can do all things through Christ which strengtheneth me."
—Philippians 4:11–13

It is a problem in mechanics how to adjust metal structures to all changes of temperature. The steel girders of a great bridge expand and contract several inches, so that they would lose their bearings on the pillars that support them with the alternate changes of summer and winter. The engineers have adjusted a simple scheme by which the sections of these girders slip past each other and adjust themselves to the changing temperature.

Human nature has never been able to discover any ethical principle sufficiently universal and strong to enable man's temper to adjust itself to the vicissitudes of life. The glory of the grace of God is that it raises us above circumstances and conditions and enables us to say with the apostle, *"I have learned, in whatsoever state I am, therewith to be content."*

The word *"content"* here is a peculiar expression, signifying the containing of his resources within his own soul so that he is not dependent on outside conditions for his happiness. His heaven is in his heart and not in his money or his friends.

The apostle was a distinguished example of perfect adjustment. He tells us that God made him a spectacle and gazing stock to both worlds. He seems to have lived his life in order to show how perfectly the grace of God could be sufficient for a man under all the varying conditions of life. Often he was abased, hungry, and apparently overwhelmed, but always without discouragement. At other times, he was called to abound and his cup was running over. But again it was without elation or selfishness. It was the testimony of one of the saints of God, and it is indeed a glorious pattern. "Once I had every earthly good, but God taught me to have God in everything. Now I have no earthly goods, but still God teaches me to have everything in God."

Not suddenly or easily did the apostle reach this victorious place. *"I have learned"* (Philippians 4:11), he said; "I have been instructed"; or, as the American Standard Version expresses it, *"I learned the secret."*

And that secret was, *"I can do all things through Christ which strengtheneth me"* (Philippians 4:13). The indwelling Christ, Himself the source of all content and happiness, will make us equal to all the changes of life.

But even this must be slowly and carefully practiced, and the Holy Spirit instructs us patiently in the art of triumphing over circumstances, glorying in tribulation, and always rejoicing in God. Let us be willing to go with Him through the school of trial and thus learn to be *"more than conquerors."*

DAY NINETEEN:

GETTING THE BEST OF PEOPLE

"Paul, called to be an apostle of Jesus Christ through the will of God, and Sosthenes our brother."
—1 Corinthians 1:1

Among the most trying difficulties and conflicts of many of our lives is the question of getting on with people. The Lord has many peculiar people, and some of us think that we have more than our share of them in our set. There is nothing that more closely tests Christian love than the unreasonableness, unkindness, and often injustice of our fellow men, and sometimes of our fellow Christians. But the resources of grace are equal to all these tests, and the love of Christ is able to triumph over people as well as over Satan and sin.

The name *Sosthenes* in our text suggests a little romance in the life of the apostle Paul. We have to read between the lines to trace the story, but it is worth all our pains. In the eighteenth chapter of Acts, we read of an attack that was made upon the apostle by the persecuting Jews at Corinth under the leadership of Sosthenes, the chief ruler of the synagogue. This man and his followers appear to have been the more violent because the previous ruler of the synagogue, Crispus, had been converted through the preaching of

Paul and *"believed on the Lord with all his house; and many of the Corinthians hearing believed, and were baptized"* (Acts 18:8). Led by Sosthenes, a Jewish mob made insurrection against Paul and dragged him to the judgment seat of Galleo, who had just arrived as the new deputy of Achia. Paul had just received a glorious promise of protection from the Lord: *"Be not afraid, but speak, and hold not thy peace: for I am with thee, and no man shall set on thee to hurt thee: for I have much people in this city"* (Acts 18:9–10).

This was signally fulfilled on the present occasion, for Galleo refused to entertain the charges of the Jews or even permit Paul to say a word in his own defense, but he drove Sosthenes and his followers from his judgment seat. Immediately the mob turned on Sosthenes and beat him in the presence of the magistrate. Thus Paul was gloriously vindicated and God's promise fulfilled. The narrative in Acts stops here. But five years later, we find Paul writing to the church in Corinth that had been through all this experience and remembered every circumstance and united with him in his greetings to them: *"Sosthenes our brother"* (1 Corinthians 1:1). This pronoun seems to point to Sosthenes as a marked character that everybody knew. How natural it is to believe that he was the very man who had once attacked Paul but is now united with him in service and sending his greetings to his old friends in Corinth. Would it be venturing too far on the wings of modest imagination to assume that after Sosthenes received his merciless beating that day in Corinth, Paul, who had just been vindicated, stepped in and interceded for him and took him under his protection, and, through the grace of God and the love of the apostle, this bitter enemy was changed to a devoted friend and became afterward the fellow laborer with the man he had once tried to destroy? Certainly this would be just like the grace of God, and we can imagine no other explanation fitting in the circumstances already stated in the narrative.

This is the love that makes us more than conquerors. We can so subdue our enemies as to destroy them. A good Quaker once said that he killed all his enemies by loving them to death. And many of us have heard the story of the Quaker farmer who led back his neighbor's cows after they had destroyed his garden, saying, "Friend, I have brought thee back thy cows after they have eaten up my corn, and I want to tell thee that if I ever catch them in my field again, I will—."

At this point, the angry owner of the cows interrupted him with, "You will, will you."

"Yes," continued the Quaker, "if I ever catch them there again, I will just bring them back to thee."

Needless to say, the feud was over and the cornfield was safe for the future.

DAY TWENTY:

TURNING EVERYTHING TO ACCOUNT FOR GOD

"It shall turn to you for a testimony."
—Luke 21:13

The Lord had been telling His disciples of the persecutions and trials that would come to them in His service. They were to be brought before kings and rulers for His name's sake. To most of us, such a situation would seem to be a great calamity, and we would be tempted to be chiefly concerned how to get out of our trouble. But He tells them to take no thought about this and to leave all matters regarding their defense to His protection, regarding the situation wholly as an opportunity for service and testimony to the gospel. *"It shall turn to you for a testimony."*

So we find the apostles in the opening chapters of the Acts in precisely this situation. They are summoned before the council and asked to explain their daring ministry. Immediately we find Peter and John ignoring all questions of their own safety and replying, *"Whether it be right in the sight of God to hearken unto you more than unto God, judge ye. For we cannot but speak the things which we have seen and heard"* (Acts 4:19–20). Paul obtained many of his best opportunities of preaching the gospel through being arrested and being brought before councils and kings. Standing before a howling mob in Jerusalem or in the presence of Felix, Festus, and

Agrippa, his one concern was to be true to his testimony. On the tossing vessel in the Adriatic Sea, amid the wild fury of the euroclydon, we find him unconcerned about his danger and thinking only of the crew and speaking the message of encouragement to them. In the last chapter of 2 Timothy, we have a splendid picture of his audience with Nero. Brought before the powerful and cruel emperor, he might almost have been pardoned for some timidity and anxiety, for the lions of the coliseum were waiting to devour him if his sentence had been adverse. But he forgets all about these personal considerations, and his own concern is to make the most of this great opportunity to preach the gospel to bloody Nero and his courtiers, which may never come to him again. Read his own account of the incident:

> At my first answer no man stood with me, but all men forsook me...Notwithstanding the Lord stood with me, and strengthened me; that by me the preaching might be fully known, and that all the Gentiles might hear.   (2 Timothy 4:16–17)

And then incidentally he adds, as of less importance, "*And I was delivered out of the mouth of the lion*" (2 Timothy 4:16–17). His business was to make the preaching fully known and have this turn to him for a testimony. It was his Master's business to deliver him from the mouth of the lion.

This is the way to be more than conquerors amid all adverse conditions and trying circumstances. Let us forget ourselves and look upon the occasion as an opportunity for service and testimony. John Vassar used to say that there were no accidents in this life but that even seeming mistakes happened that he might tell somebody of the Savior. On one occasion, he knocked at a door and found that he was at the wrong house. As the lady opened the door and he explained his mistake, he courteously apologized and then added, "Perhaps, Madam, there was no mistake. It may be the Lord permitted me to call that I might give to you the message that was intended for another. May I come in and talk with you for a few minutes?" The result was the salvation of her soul. It "turned to him for a testimony." Is our life thus witnessing always and all for God?

DAY TWENTY-ONE:

THE DOUBLE PORTION

"I pray thee, let a double portion of thy spirit be upon me."
—2 Kings 2:9

W e are hardly justified in interpreting this prayer in the light of our modern theology and of what we now know of the doctrine of the Holy Spirit. All this was as yet unrevealed to Elisha. We must, therefore, interpret this prayer in the light of the facts through which it was answered, for he was told that his petition should be granted upon certain conditions that were fulfilled. We may be assured, therefore, that the double portion, whatever it meant, did come to him.

What does the life and ministry that follows teach us about this great blessing, and in what sense may we intelligently repeat the prayer and expect its fulfillment?

In the first place, the life which followed was a normal and simple one. There was no strain about it as in the case of Elijah. It was a life among the people filled out in all the relationships of life and all the environment of our commonplace experiences.

But in the next place, interwoven through all these experiences, was a golden thread of the supernatural, the divine. While the things were not in themselves extraordinary, they were done in an extraordinary way. And so the double portion of the Spirit brings to us a life all interpenetrated with the presence and the mighty working of the living God.

The first experience that met Elisha after his blessing was an impossible difficulty and an impassable barrier. The Jordan crossed his path, and his work lay beyond. A few hours before, he had Elijah to bid the waters divide; but now he faced it alone. This was his first test, and he met it by simple faith and by counting upon the blessing that he had just received, showing his faith by his works. He did not ask for Elijah, but he called upon the God of Elijah; and the waters divided, and the sons of the prophet knew that the spirit of Elijah did rest upon Elisha.

His next experience was a great public emergency. The armies of his country and their allies were perishing from water famine in the mountains of Moab. Again he claimed the potency of the double portion, and the answer was, *"Ye shall not see wind, neither shall ye see rain; yet that valley shall be filled with water....And this is but a light thing in the sight of the LORD: he will deliver the Moabites also into your hand"* (2 Kings 3:17–18).

The next illustration is found in the beautiful story of the widow's pot of oil. It is too long to follow in detail, but the lesson is that the Holy Spirit, whom we have received but often fail to use, can be poured into every vessel of need in our life and become as real as our difficulties and necessities.

Later, we see Elisha's blessing operating in the healing of Naaman, not through Elisha's touch, but through Naaman's own faith; and we learn that the baptism of the Spirit means the quickening of our bodies according to our faith.

Yet again we find the prophet in imminent danger and surrounded by the squadrons who had come to capture him. Elisha has learned the confidence which banishes all fear, but his servant was in dismay. And so the prophet asks that his eyes may be opened, and, lo, he sees the hosts of the heavenly cavalry encamped around them on every side and arrayed against their foes. So the fullness of the Spirit becomes our resource in danger and our sure defense against every foe.

How beautiful the story of the rescue of the borrowed axe in the little student hand by the Jordan! A touch of faith and the lost iron rose and floated on the surface of the water. How simply and sublimely it reminds us of that supernatural power that can lift us above natural and spiritual forces and prove that our divine Leader is head over all things for His trusting people!

And so the story moves on with its record of divine all-sufficiency, and yet at every point, it touches our life today and reminds us that the same God is able to make all grace abound unto us, so *"that [we], always having all sufficiency in all things, may abound to every good work"* (2 Corinthians 9:8).

DAY TWENTY-TWO:

CALEB'S INHERITANCE

*"If so be the Lord will be with me, then I shall be able to
drive them out, as the Lord said."*
—Joshua 14:12

This was the heroic testimony of an aged veteran on his eighty-fifth birthday, when ordinary men would be supposed to have long ago retired from active service and be waiting for their translation. But Caleb was only just beginning the most serious business of life. His greatest ambition and His grandest achievement still lay before him, and he asked as a birthday present the opportunity of doing the hardest thing that any of his people had ever attempted. This was nothing less than the capture of Hebron, the stronghold of the sons of Anak.

How it is fitted to inspire us with some of that kind of faith of which we read in the eleventh chapter of Hebrews, the faith that *"subdued kingdoms, wrought righteousness, obtained promises…out of weakness [was] made strong, waxed valiant in fight, turned to flight the armies of the aliens"* (Hebrews 11:33–34).

Is there anyone reading these lines who has begun to count his life work over and to shirk the hard places and the heavy burdens and battles of life? Think of Caleb and Hebron and do not miss life's crowning victories. The best is yet to come if your faith will only dare to claim it.

The conquest of Hebron meant something more than the ordinary achievements of a life of faith. They had already conquered the land and gained the common inheritance of Israel. Hebron meant an extra heritage, one of the special prizes in the struggle of faith. So God has for all who are willing to be baptized with the baptism of suffering and drink of the cup of trial a special recompense of reward. It was Paul's ambition to win a crown and to accomplish a service that others had failed to do. There is a place for holy ambition. The later chapters of the book of Joshua tell us of these choice possessions awaiting courageous faith. Caleb's was perhaps the greatest of them all.

Again, this victorious achievement meant a hard fight and a powerful and relentless foe. It was the very citadel of the Anakim, the giant rulers of Canaan. These men stood for the strength of evil in the human heart, the life of self and sin in all its rudiments and ramifications. No great prize is won without opposition and difficulty. The devil does not take much trouble with ordinary people. He reserves his best shots for the most valuable game. We read that as soon as David was crowned king of Hebron, the Philistines came up to seek David. He had suddenly become an object of interest to them because he had become a king. And so when we are pressing on for the highest things, we shall always find the principalities and powers not on the lower planes of life but in the heavenly places.

The story is told about a regiment that had been punished for an ignominious defeat by the loss of their colors. They were deeply humiliated and eagerly awaited the chance to retrieve their failure. At last, it came. One day, the commander called them and, pointing to a rugged hill bristling with the artillery of the enemy, said, "Boys, there are your colors. Go and get them." It needed no second word to start that resistless charge. And they came back bloodstained but triumphant with their flag wrested from the grip of their most powerful enemies. Our flags of honor and our crowns of glory are waiting us yonder on many a height of difficulty and danger. Shall we be found in the ranks of Caleb and on the heights of Hebron?

A deep spiritual suggestion lies back of the name of Hebron. It was the place made sacred by the abode of Abraham, the friend of God, and in Arabic the name means "the friend." It stands for the victory of love in our spiritual arena. And perhaps there is no higher or harder citadel of spiritual conflict and aspiration. The severest tests of our Christian life come to us along the line of love that suffers long and is still kind, and the charity that *"beareth all things, believeth all things, hopeth all things, endureth all things"* (1 Corinthians 13:7). And this kind of love is not won by mere endeavor. It is not the result of ethical culture but the victory of faith. What an insight those disciples had when, after listening to the Lord's high standard of the love He expected from them and the forgiveness that could reach not merely seven times but seventy times seven, they looked up to Him in conscious helplessness and cried to the Lord, *"Increase our faith"* (Luke 17:5). Why did they not ask the Lord to increase their love? They were beginning to understand the faith that works by love.

Beloved, let us follow Caleb and win our Hebron.

DAY TWENTY-THREE:

TRUE GREATNESS

"Thou art a great people...thou shalt not have one lot only:
but the mountain shall be thine...for thou shalt drive out
the Canaanites, though they have iron chariots,
and though they be strong."
—Joshua 17:17–18

There is a fine touch of humor as well as truth in the dramatic story of the meeting between the sons of Joseph and Joshua. These men were not unlike another company of sons in later Hebrew history, the sons of Zebedee, who came with their mother to Christ, asking for the choice seats in the future kingdom, and who got an answer not unlike the one that Joshua gave to his interviewers. The men of Ephraim and Manasseh came to Joshua when the tribes were receiving their inheritances and asked for a double portion and a choice inheritance because, they said, *"I am a great people, for-asmuch as the LORD hath blessed me hitherto"* (Joshua 17:14). Joshua did not deny their self-confident claim. He quietly answered with a fine touch of sarcasm, *"If thou be a great people, then get thee up to the wood country, and cut down for thyself there in the land of the Perizzites and of the giants, if mount Ephraim be too narrow for thee"* (verse 15).

It must be said for them that they met the challenge bravely and won the prize in the face of overwhelming odds. These was

the speed of the enemy. They had iron chariots and were strong.
But the men of Ephraim drove them out, and they won their great
inheritance and became the most powerful of the northern tribes in
all the coming centuries, so that, for a while, the name of Ephraim
was actually given to the whole kingdom of the ten tribes.

When the sons of Zebedee came to Christ with their similar ambition, He did not frown upon their lofty aspirations or tell
them they were too ambitious. He simply reminded them that
these prizes were not given by partiality or personal preference but
were won by sacrifice and service. *"To sit on my right hand and on
my left hand is not mine to give; but it shall be given to them for whom
it is prepared"* (Mark 10:40). And He asks significantly, *"Can ye
drink of the cup that I drink of? and be baptized with the baptism that
I am baptized with?"* (verse 38). They did not shrink from the heart-
searching test, and we believe they did not miss the costly prize.

Beloved, life is what we make it. Our crowns or chains are
forged in the workshop of life. Our future harvest is the outgrowth
of our earthly sowing. The man of time is the immortal of eternity.
He who is unjust shall be unjust still; he who is righteous shall be
righteous still; he who is holy shall be holy still. The story is perhaps familiar of the lady who dreamt that she was in heaven and
that an angel was showing her the city. A beautiful mansion was
pointed out, and she eagerly asked the name of the happy owner.
"Oh," said the angel, "it belongs to a man from your town, in New
York State."

As soon as she heard the name, she said, "Why, that is our
gardener; what could he ever do with such a mansion? He lives in
a lodge in three little rooms. He has no culture and spends most of
his evening in the Salvation Army meetings."

"Well," said the angel, "I do not understand these things, but I
am sure the Master knows what He is doing."

Then they came to a very modest little dwelling, and with a look of deference, the angel said, "That is the home that is being prepared for you."

"Oh," she said, "there must be some mistake. That would suit the gardener much better, and his must be intended for me."

"No," said the angel, "there is no mistake, and I think the explanation must be that the Master does the best He can with the materials the people send up here."

Dear friend, what sort of materials are we sending up there? Here again the test of greatness and the secret of reward is difficulty, opposition, conflict, and sacrifice. These hills were crowned with mighty forests that had to be cut down and defended by chariots of iron that had to be driven out. All precious things are guarded by obstacles and adverse conditions. Even the kernel of the nut is hidden in a rugged shell. The gem is buried in the rocks and mountains. The pearl is found in ocean depths. And in the spiritual world, the richest prizes must be wrested from the hardest places. The great apostle Paul would not allow a single self-denial or sacrifice to be abated because he believed that there was no glory in merely preaching the gospel. The only way he could win a crown was by preaching it without charge and bearing a double share of sacrifice and hardship.

We do not need to look for these hard places. God will send them as we are able to bear them; and if our reliance is upon Him, we can say with Caleb and the men of Ephraim, *"If so be the Lord will be with me, then I shall be able to drive them out, as the Lord said"* (Joshua 14:12).

DAY TWENTY-FOUR:

LAST STRONGHOLDS

"Nevertheless David took the strong hold of Zion."
—2 Samuel 5:7

After the conquest of Canaan by Joshua and all the victories of Saul and David, there had still remained four hundred years one stronghold in the hands of the Canaanites. It was the old city of Jebus, afterward Jerusalem, the capital of the Jebusites. This citadel was naturally impregnable and even after David's coronation refused to yield to his sway. Indeed, so confident were the Jebusites of their security in their natural fortress that they sent a challenge to David telling him that Jebus was defended by a lot of old blind cripples and that he would have to drive them out before he could capture it. The challenge was answered by Joab, and Jebus was captured by him; and for his brave achievement, he was rewarded with the post of commander in chief of the armies of Israel. Jebus immediately became the castle of David and the citadel of Jerusalem. That which had been the stronghold of the enemy up to the very last moment was henceforth to become the seat of divine dominion not only in the history of Israel but in that more glorious age when Mount Zion shall be the metropolis of the millennial world. What a splendid transformation!

What a suggestive lesson this story has for spiritual eyes that are opened to see our own hearts, our failures, and our possibilities of victory and attainment.

In the first place, there may still be something lurking in our hearts and lives that has not been wholly yielded up or won for Christ. We have left a Jericho behind us, or a Jebus in the very center of our spiritual world. There is an enemy in the citadel. We have had victory over all our old habits but one. That besetting sin still lingers and claims the right to be tolerated and spared. Perhaps it is some infirmity of temper that we call trifling, some pet indulgence that we suffer to remain, some neglected duty in the closet or the family altar, some omission in our Christian service for others, some old wrong that has never been righted and perhaps forgotten, or some failure to enter into our full inheritance. Perhaps it is a physical weakness that we have not claimed the power to overcome, or some long-forgotten promise or vow that we have not yet fulfilled. Memory and conscience, if we will ask the Lord to quicken them, will help us to locate our Jebus; and the Holy Spirit will convict us of the danger and the sin of allowing the flag of the enemy to still float even in a single neglected corner of his inheritance.

Satan is perfectly willing to let us have everything else if we will just give him standing room in one spot. They tell of a Hindu prince that had a great ambition to own a splendid estate. But one poor man held the title to an obscure corner lot, and, although offered millions, he refused to sell it. It was his pride and the prince's constant chagrin for him to be able to say, "Remember, Your Excellency, that you and I own the town." Satan is quite satisfied if he can say that to our blessed Master.

Sometimes our Jebus is held by the blind and the lame like the Canaanite stronghold of old. The victory would not be hard if we but dared to face it as Joab did. It is only the long habits of tolerance, indolence, and unfaithfulness that have entrenched the foe. Shall we arise and drive him out and be all the Lord's?

The inspiring lesson of our text is that the things that have been most hardly won from the enemy and most shamefully used by him against our Lord and ourselves are the things that God wants to choose and use for His highest glory. It was this Jebus that became the metropolis of Israel and is yet to be the height of Zion and the site of the palace of the King. And so it is the things that have cost us most that God wants to use for noblest service. Shall you let Him have that last stronghold of your life of self and sin and through it magnify His grace and glorify His name?

And so we have seen Him in our day take the victim of a life of dissipation and make him the herald of salvation to countless fellow sufferers and sinners. So, late perhaps in life, some lingering infirmity has been overcome, some victory won over natural or spiritual disability, and a life transformed and filled with the Holy Spirit has become the instrument of the noblest triumphs of the cross. So Christ is waiting, dear friend, to take the hardest, saddest thing in your defeated life and make your Jebus His Jerusalem.

DAY TWENTY-FIVE:

EFFECTUAL PRAYER

"Thou shouldest have smitten five or six times."
—2 Kings 13:19

The story of Elisha closes with a dramatic scene by his deathbed. Jehoash, the king of Israel, had come to pay his last respects to the venerable prophet, and Elisha saluted him with the cry, *"My father, my father, the chariot of Israel, and the horsemen thereof"* (2 Kings 2:12). Then Elisha answered the wicked but kindhearted king by giving him an object lesson of the real secret which had inspired his life and which might still be the resource of Jehoash and Israel. He bade him bring a bow and arrow and shoot the arrows through the open window toward the East in the direction of Damascus and Syria. Meanwhile the prophet's hands were upon the hands of the king as he pulled the string and aimed the arrows. Then he exclaimed, *"The arrow of the deliverance from Syria"* (2 Kings 13:17). This was a vivid expression of the power of believing prayer. How vividly the pointed arrow suggests the definiteness of prayer! The promise is not only "all things" but *"whatsoever ye shall ask in my name, that will I do"* (John 14:13). The spring of the bow represents the impulse of faith. And the hand of the prophet upon that of the king reminds us of the intercession of the Lord Jesus Christ for us and His fellowship in all true prayer.

It would seem as if the promised blessing were now assured. But, no. There must next come the test and proving of individual faith. The first act was not wholly due to the faith of the king, for he was largely under the influence of another spirit. Now he must show his own faith and win his own victory. God tests our prayers, and when they come through the crucible, there often is but little left of all that passed our impulsive lips.

So the prophet commands,

Take the arrows. And he took them. And he said unto the king of Israel, Smite upon the ground. And he smote thrice, and stayed. And the man of God was wroth with him, and said, Thou shouldest have smitten five or six times; then hadst thou smitten Syria till thou hadst consumed it: whereas now thou shalt smite Syria but thrice.   (2 Kings 13:18–19)

How striking and eloquent the message of these words! Jehoash thought he had done very well when he duplicated and triplicated what to him was certainly an extraordinary act of faith. But the Lord and the prophet were bitterly disappointed because he had stopped halfway. He got something. He got much. He got exactly what he believed for in the final test, but he did not get all that the prophet meant and the Lord wanted to bestow. He missed much of the meaning of the promise and the fullness of the blessing. He reached the comparative but not the superlative of life. He got something better than the human, but he did not get God's best.

Beloved, how solemn is the application! How heart-searching the message of God to us! How important that we should learn to pray through! Elisha had learned this well when he was seeking the double portion. The prophet had tested him to the very depths, and again and again he had sought to dissuade him from his purpose and turn him aside at Gilgal, Bethel, Jericho, and Jordan. But Elisha had persistently replied, *"As the Lord liveth, and as thy soul liveth, I will not leave thee"* (2 Kings 2:2). It was this that brought him the blessing of his life, and it is the lack of this that leaves so many prayers unanswered and so many purposes broken off.

How solemn is the test that God is always making of our hearts! *"What is man,"* the patriarch cried unto the Lord, *"that thou shouldest magnify him? and that thou shouldest set thine heart upon him? And that thou shouldest visit him every morning, and try him every moment?"* (Job 7:17–18). Looking upon the Syrophoenician mother, the words of Christ seemed harsh as He again and again beat back her supplication and her plea. But all the while, He was watching her indestructible faith even as the refiner watches the molten gold in the cleansing flame; and when at last she had prayed through and could not be repulsed, He cried, *"O woman, great is thy faith: be it unto thee even as thou wilt"* (Matthew 15:28).

Beloved, shall we claim all the fullness of the promise and all the possibilities of believing prayer?

DAY TWENTY-SIX:

FAITH'S CHALLENGE

"There is nothing too hard for thee."
—Jeremiah 32:17

"Is there any thing too hard for me?"
—Jeremiah 32:27

*"Call unto me, and I will answer thee, and show thee great
and mighty things, which thou knowest not."*
—Jeremiah 33:3

In the darkest hour of old Jerusalem, there came to Jeremiah the hardest test of faith. Real estate was worthless, for the Chaldeans were encamped in all the land, and Jeremiah knew that the city itself was about to fall. It was then that God appeared to the prophet and commanded him to invest his fortune, perhaps all that he had, in a piece of real estate outside the doomed city in his old village home at Anathoth. It was surely the wildest speculation that any man ever ventured on. But God told him to do it as an act of faith in the future restoration of the land, and as he obeyed, Jehovah added the promise *"Houses and fields and vineyards shall be possessed again in this land"* (Jeremiah 32:15).

The prophet obeyed the strange command in an act of faith, and then he began the prayer of faith. We cannot pray the prayer of faith till we have already committed ourselves to the act that proves our faith. This was the way He prayed: *"Ah Lord God! behold, thou hast made the heaven and the earth by thy great power and stretched out arm, and there is nothing too hard for thee"* (Jeremiah 32:17). There is no evolution here. Evolution is a poor place for faith. We have to believe in a God that can make things out of nothing before our prayers can go very far.

Like an echo, the answer comes back, *"Behold, I am the Lord, the God of all flesh: is there any thing too hard for me?"* (Jeremiah 32:27). The word *Anathoth* has a beautiful connection here. It means "echo," and it suggests that faith is just an echo of God. And so Jehovah continues to tell the prophet how He will fulfill his prayer and exceed his expectations in the blessings that are to come.

Our third text is the climax of this glorious divine message: *"Call unto me, and I will answer thee, and show thee great and mighty things, which thou knowest not"* (Jeremiah 33:3). It is a fine summary of the highest kind of prayer.

First, it encourages us to ask the greatest things from God. It lifts us up into the realm of celestial magnitudes and the magnificence of God's resources. It is easier for God to do great and difficult things than something easy and trifling. Faith honors Him by counting upon His infinite resources. When the favorite of Alexander asked him for something almost worth a kingdom, the emperor replied, "It may be too much for Parmento to ask, but it is not too much for Alexander to give." "Pray for the impossible" may seem too bold and startling, and yet it is not bolder than the Master's words *"with God all things are possible"* (Matthew 19:26). *"All things are possible to him that believeth"* (Mark 9:23).

Next, it bids us go to God for things entirely beyond our past experiences and our previous standards. He bids us ask for hidden things that we know not. We are constantly moving in a circle.

He wants us to break that monotony and rise to new planes, standards, ideals, ventures, in that immensity that *"eye hath not seen, nor ear heard, neither have entered into the heart of man, the things which God hath prepared for them that love him"* (1 Corinthians 2:9).

Once more, He tells us that He will answer us. That undoubtedly refers to the message that His Spirit will first bring to our heart and our faith. He will give us the assurance of the answer, and He bids us believe that we do receive the things that we ask without waiting to see it in actual fulfillment.

Finally, He promises after He has answered to show us in actual realization and manifestation all that we believe for. The first of these promises is the message over the telephone. The second is the delivery wagon bringing the promised blessing. Too often, we wait like Jacob to see Joseph's wagons before we fully believe in Joseph and are at rest about our blessing. May the Holy Spirit lift us up to the largeness of God and enable us to hear the Master pleading, *"Hitherto have ye asked nothing in my name: ask, and ye shall receive, that your joy may be full"* (John 16:24).

DAY TWENTY-SEVEN:

HOW GREAT IS YOUR GOD?

"I am the Almighty God; walk before me, and be thou perfect."
—Genesis 17:1

The glorious name that Jehovah here assumes is literally El Shaddai, the all-sufficient One, "the God who is enough" as Matthew Henry happily translates it.

The great question that determines the magnitude of every life is the kind of God we have. The man who has a limited God will have a limited experience. The man who has caught the vision of El Shaddai will live up to that glorious standard. Let us not look so much at ourselves and try to pull ourselves up to a higher plane, as someone has said, by our bootstraps; but let us look up to the God who is calling to us from on high, until, like a mighty magnet, He attracts us to His own transcendent plans.

It was the revelation and realization of God that made Abraham the great discoverer of new worlds of faith and vision, the Christopher Columbus, as someone has said, of spiritual discovery.

Beloved friend, how large a God have you?

1. Abraham's God was sufficient to enable him to give up his home, country, and earthly prospects and go forth to a new world with nothing but God. And the vision of such a

God will enable us to turn our backs upon the present evil age and find our portion and inheritance in Him.

2. Abraham's God was sufficient to enable him once more to renounce and let go all present earthly prospects when the selfishness of Lot demanded the best part of Abraham's inheritance. Instead of wrangling with his unworthy nephew, he let him take his choice and kept what Lot left. And then God came to him that night and told him that all the land, including Lot's portion, should be his inheritance forever. So when we once get the vision of the greatness of our God, it is easy to let the world go by and wait for our portion from Him.

3. Abraham's God was sufficient to inspire him with faith and courage to defend his inheritance from the enemy and go forth against the allied armies of the East when they invaded the land. What a daring attack that was, and what a magnificent victory, reminding one of Oliver Cromwell or Stonewall Jackson. It was faith that prompted the enterprise and won the victory. He did not resist Lot's selfishness, but he did resist the common foe. So faith will lead us to defend our covenant rights from the great adversary and to refuse to give place to the devil at any point.

4. Abraham's God was sufficient to enable him to believe the promise of his seed, to confess his faith when it seemed impossible, and to wait a quarter of a century for its fulfillment. The very name he took, Abraham, was a confession of his confidence in the birth of Isaac, when he was past age and it was contrary to all natural probability that he should have a son. So faith still counts the things that are not as if they were because it has a God that can create things out of nothing and discount the future as if it were the past.

5. Abraham's God enabled him to give up even the child of promise at God's call and trust in the face of every seeming contradiction that the promise would be fulfilled notwithstanding. All Abraham's faith and future were centered in Isaac and yet God bade him lay him on the altar. He could not see how it was possible, humanly, for Isaac to be sacrificed and the covenant fulfilled. But he simply obeyed believing that His God was able to raise him even from the dead, and his faith was honored and his love accepted, as God witnessed: *"Now I know that thou fearest God, seeing thou hast not withheld thy son, thine only son from me"* (Genesis 22:12). So we can give our best to God when we realize that the God who claims the sacrifice is able to give us ten thousand times as much in return.

6. Abraham's confidence in God enabled him to make intercession for the cities of the plain and to win the glorious name of "the friend of God." Beloved, how large is our God, and can we say that He is our Friend?

DAY TWENTY-EIGHT:

A LARGER VISION

"Lift up now thine eyes, and look from the place where thou art...for all the land which thou seest, to thee will I give it."
—Genesis 13:14–15

It has been finely said:

> Gideons must Isaiahs be,
> Vision first, then victory![6]

The apostle Paul has repeated this thought in 1 Corinthians 2:12: *"We have received...the spirit which is of God; that we might know the things that are freely given to us of God."* A larger vision leads to a larger faith and experience. The Interpreter takes us through all the Palace Beautiful and then, having shown us all its chambers and its treasures, He hands us the key, declaring, "All that thou seest is thine."[7] Let us ask God, therefore, to give us the largest possible vision of our spiritual inheritance.

This is the thought underlying the great epistle to the Ephesians. After the reference to the sealing of the Spirit, Paul immediately prays that we may have *"the spirit of wisdom and revelation in the knowledge of him: the eyes of your understanding being*

---

6. Charles A. Fox, "Gideon's Cry."
7. Anna Laetitia Barbauld, "A Hymn," *The Works of Anna Laetitia Barbauld*, vol. 2 (New York: Sleight & Tucker, 1826), 350.

enlightened; that ye may know…the exceeding greatness of his power to us-ward who believe" (Ephesians 1:17–19). Then he proceeds to lead us into the experience of the vision, until it culminates in the exhortation "Be filled with the Spirit" (Ephesians 5:18).

Hagar, weeping in the wilderness in deep despair, needs only to have her eyes opened to behold the well that was already there and to find all her wants supplied. Abraham, raising the knife to slay his son on Mount Moriah,

> …lifted up his eyes, and looked, and behold behind him a ram caught in a thicket by his horns: and Abraham went and took the ram, and offered him up for a burnt offering in the stead of his son. And Abraham called the name of that place Jehovahjireh: as it is said to this day, in the mount of the LORD it shall be seen.   (Genesis 22:13–14)

He, too, had seen a vision of which Christ afterward spoke, "Your father Abraham rejoiced to see my day: and he saw it, and was glad" (John 8:56). Still faith needs to be divinely illumined to "behold the Lamb of God, which taketh away the sin of the world" (John 1:29).

Moses, standing at Marah amid the murmurings of the people who could not drink of the bitter waters, "cried unto the LORD; and the LORD shewed him a tree, which when he had cast into the waters, the waters were made sweet" (Exodus 15:25). That branch of healing is still beside us; but, oh, how many there are that never see it, and suffer and sink in disease and death along the way.

Elisha on the mount, surrounded by the cavalry of the Syrians, lifts up his head with triumph while his servant is wailing in dismay. And the prophet simply asks the Lord to open his eyes and let him see the chariots of God encamped around them in their defense.

Again the apostle tells us how the wise and cultured of this world esteem the gospel as foolishness and lose the vision of the Christ because *"eye hath not seen, nor ear heard, neither have entered into the heart of man, the things which God hath prepared for them that love him. But God hath revealed them unto us by his Spirit"* (1 Corinthians 2:9–10) and *"we have received…the spirit which is of God; that we might know the things that are freely given to us of God"* (verse 12).

So God is calling us to lift up our eyes and behold the vision of our land of promise. Let us look northward and southward and eastward and westward. Northward are stormy winds and desolate wastes, but God is there in His all-sufficient grace. Southward are burning sands and scorching suns. But there faith can see the upper and the nether springs. Eastward is the sunrise of the great unknown future. But there we may behold the vision of the Lamb opening the seals of life and preparing for us all the riches of the glory of His inheritance in the saints and waiting to guide us into our promised land. And westward lie the setting sun and the shadows of the eventide and the darkness of the night. But to the vision of faith, *"at evening time it shall be light"* (Zechariah 14:7) and *"there shall be no night there"* (Revelation 22:5). Let us take in all the land and then let us hear Him say, *"All the land which thou seest, to thee will I give it"* (Genesis 13:15); and someday, we shall be able to say, "Nothing failed of all that the Lord had spoken; all came to pass." (See Joshua 21:45.)

DAY TWENTY-NINE:

A GREAT AMBITION

"Having hope…to preach the gospel in the regions beyond you."
—2 Corinthians 10:15–16

The superlative of life means much more than a Christian experience terminating on itself and bounded by the narrow limits of its own blessing. The wellspring in the fourth chapter of the gospel of John becomes rivers of living water when it begins to flow out to other lives.

Our text speaks of a noble ambition on the part of the great apostle to reach beyond all selfish limitations to the needs of others, and even yet further to the largest of all needs, the need of a lost heathen world. Yes, and still further does his ambition stretch to the most destitute and neglected parts even of this desolate field. He wants to go where no other feet have gone and to tell the story where no other voice has witnessed of the redeeming love and precious blood of His blessed Master. And that ambition never rested until it had reached its goal and he could say in the hearing of countless living witnesses,

From Jerusalem, and round about Illyricum, I have fully preached the gospel of Christ. Yea, so have I strived to preach the gospel, not where Christ was named, lest I should build upon another man's foundation: but as it is written, To whom

*he was not spoken of, they shall see: and they that have not
heard shall understand.*   (Romans 15:19–21)

Here we have the picture of a sublime ambition: first, to live
an unselfish life that reaches beyond himself; second, to carry the
gospel to the heathen world; and third, even in this to go to the
regions beyond where others have not gone.

This has been truly called the greatest work in the world.
We are justified in regarding such an ambition as the noblest of
all divine passions. Would to God that passion might be kindled
afresh in the heart of someone who reads these lines.

1.   Consider the magnificence of the missionary enterprise, its
     glorious history, its hallowed associations, the noble names
     of missionaries and martyrs that have been identified with
     it, the vast scope of its plan and program, the untold bless-
     ings that it brings even on the human plane to suffering
     humanity, and the glorious message of salvation, life, and
     eternal hope that it carries. What work can be compared
     with this in loftiness and attraction to every noble nature?

2.   Consider the awful need of the world. Even on the secular
     plane, the gospel is the highest and best remedy for the
     curse of heathenism; the shame of womanhood; the blight
     of childhood; the opium curse of China; the witch doctor
     of Africa; the poverty of India; and the ignorance, degra-
     dation, and misery of a thousand millions of our fellow
     beings. But the gospel is the only remedy for their spiritual
     destitution and their religious need. All human religions
     fail to bridge the gulf between man and God, and to us
     as the disciples of Christ has been given the only message
     that can give one chance of eternal life to every human
     soul. What a sacred trust! What an awful responsibility!
     What a sublime ambition!

3. Consider what it means to our Master's heart, for He has already made the mighty sacrifice of His own life to make this enterprise possible. He has died not only for us but for the world; and if need be, He would die again. Shall we allow that precious blood to be shed in vain, or shall we let Him see of the travail of His soul in its efficacy to save the yet unevangelized millions who wait for our message? Surely, ambition and devotion should combine to make each one of us, as much as in us is, real missionaries.

4. And consider the marvelous opportunities that the providence of God is giving us today to evangelize our own generation. All the forces of heaven and all the resources of the Holy Spirit seem to be concentrated on earth's mission fields. The seraphim are crying, *"Holy, holy, holy, is the* Lord *of hosts: the whole earth is full of his glory"* (Isaiah 6:3). God is calling, *"Whom shall I send, and who will go for us?"* (Isaiah 6:8). Oh, let it be our sublime ambition to answer quickly, "Here am I, oh, Lord, send me!" (See Isaiah 6:8.)

DAY THIRTY:

LIVING OUR BIBLES

"There failed not ought of any good thing which the Lord
had spoken unto the house of Israel; all came to pass."
—Joshua 21:45

Is it possible to translate the whole Bible into a human life and to live out in actual experience all that we know and believe?

This has been done in one human life at least. It was the continual purpose of the Lord Jesus Christ to fulfill every Scripture that had been written of Him, and He could not die until the last of these prophecies had come to pass. Again and again we read in the story of His life, "For thus must the Scripture be fulfilled." (See, for example, Matthew 26:54; Acts 1:16.) The life of the Lord Jesus was, therefore, a living Bible. Why should not our lives be the same?

The Word of God has been inspired and recorded amid every conceivable variety of human experience and touches our life at every point. Therefore, it *"is profitable for doctrine, for reproof, for correction, for instruction in righteousness: that the man of God may be perfect, thoroughly furnished unto all good works"* (2 Timothy 3:16–17). It would save us from a great deal of narrowness, shallowness, and instability if we made it the purpose of our life to possess a genuine Bible Christianity, and our high ambition to fulfill every Scripture that has been written for our profit.

For example, do we want to get correct ideas of the physical universe and the material creation? We do not need to spend our lives studying worms and apes to find this out, for *"through faith we understand that the worlds were framed by the word of God, so that things which are seen were not made of things which do appear"* (Hebrews 11:3).

Do we want to have a satisfactory assurance of our personal salvation? We turn to the last chapter of the first epistle of John and we read,

> *If we receive the witness of men, the witness of God is greater…*
> *He that believeth not God hath made him a liar; because he*
> *believeth not the record that God gave of his Son. And this is*
> *the record, that God hath given to us eternal life, and this life*
> *is in his Son. He that hath the Son hath life; and he that hath*
> *not the Son of God hath not life. These things have I written*
> *unto you that believe on the name of the Son of God; that ye*
> *may know that ye have eternal life, and that ye may believe on*
> *the name of the Son of God.*   (1 John 5:9–13)

There we find a divine foundation for the assurance of faith by simply taking God at His Word and taking the life that He freely gives us through His Son.

Are we seeking for the deeper experience of complete victory over sin and a life of holiness, peace, and power? Again we have in our own Bible the promise of the Holy Spirit, the revelation of Jesus Christ as our Sanctification and Life, and the divine assurance that it is the will of God to sanctify us through and through and that our *"whole spirit and soul and body be preserved blameless unto the coming of our Lord Jesus Christ"* (1 Thessalonians 5:23).

Are we fighting the battle of temptation? Again we are reminded that the Master met the Tempter with the sword of the Spirit, and before every thrust of the resistless words *"It is written"* (Matthew 4:4, 6–7, 10), the enemy retreated. That living Word is still our potent armor against all the wiles of the adversary.

Are we seeking direction in the perplexities of life? Again we read, *"If any of you lack wisdom, let him ask of God, that giveth to all men liberally...and it shall be given him"* (James 1:5).

Are we sick and wondering where to go for help and healing? Our Bibles meet us at once with a divine prescription, *"Is any sick among you? let him call for the elders of the church; and let them pray over him, anointing him with oil in the name of the Lord: and the prayer of faith shall save the sick, and the Lord shall raise him up"* (James 5:14–15). What a comfort it is to simply obey the Lord and leave the responsibility with Him!

Have we some trouble with a brother who has wronged us? Again, instead of telling all the neighbors and raising a cloud of reproach upon the cause of Christ, our Bible has told us exactly what to do—namely, to first deal with him privately and faithfully; and then if this fails, take one or two others with us; and then. as a last resort, appeal to the church of God. (See Matthew 18:15–17.) Thus in a thousand ways, the Word of God is a sufficient manual and guide. Are we living it out in all its promises and precepts and in all the length and breadth of our daily lives?

DAY THIRTY-ONE:

THE MASTER'S "WELL DONE"

*"That, when he shall appear, we may have confidence, and
not be ashamed before him at his coming."*
—1 John 2:28

The coming of our Lord is the blessed hope of the believer. But it is a very solemn as well as a very sweet anticipation.

Our text suggests that there are some even of His own disciples who shall be ashamed before Him at His coming. The Lord Jesus has given us the picture of the watching servants who are waiting to open to Him immediately and those who are taken by sad surprise. We read in 1 Corinthians 3:13–15 that the day when Christ returns, He will make manifest our work and try it by fire and, in that awful ordeal, the works of many shall be found to be but wood and hay and stubble and shall be dissolved in flames and leave the worker himself to be saved as by fire. We read of others who shall give account with grief and not with joy. We have the solemn pictures of the servants returning their single talent and their single pound uninvested and unimproved, and receiving not the approbation but the severest reprobation of the Lord (see Matthew 25:24–26), while the faithful servants receive His open approval and the glorious recompense of their reward (see Matthew 25:20–23).

How solemnly the apostle Paul looks forward to the rendering of his account as a witness for Christ and a steward of the gospel:

Wherefore we labour, that, whether present or absent, we may be accepted of him. For we must all appear before the judgment seat of Christ; that every one may receive the things done in his body, according to that he hath done, whether it be good or bad. Knowing therefore the terror of the Lord, we persuade men. (2 Corinthians 5:9–11).

How vigilantly he watches against every weight and sin as he runs his glorious race for an incorruptible crown! *"I therefore so run, not as uncertainly; so fight I, not as one that beateth the air: but I keep under my body, and bring it into subjection: lest that by any means, when I have preached to others, I myself should be a castaway"* (1 Corinthians 9:26–27). This word *"castaway"* has no reference to the final loss of his salvation. It literally means "disapproved" and has special reference to the verdict of the judges regarding the competitors for the prize. *"One receiveth the prize"* (1 Corinthians 9:24), while the others are *"castaway"* (verse 27) or disapproved.

The apostle Peter in the first chapter of his second epistle uses an expression that was suggested by the public arena where men contended in the race. It was at the home stretch when the goal was in full view that the greatest efforts were made both by the competitor and those who encouraged him from the galleries, and there was a special signal set up at the point where the racers turned into the home stretch on which the letters were emblazoned, "Make speed!" Peter uses a similar expression when he says, *"Wherefore the rather, brethren, give diligence [make speed] to make your calling and election sure: for if ye do these things, ye shall never fall: for so an entrance shall be ministered unto you abundantly* into the everlasting kingdom of our Lord and Saviour Jesus Christ" (2 Peter 1:10–11). Are we making sure of that abundant entrance, or shall we be *"ashamed before him at his coming"* (1 John 2:28)?

In his solemn message to the church in Philadelphia—the church that came nearest of all the seven to meeting His complete approval—the Lord Jesus Christ in His last words to the Christian age utters this significant warning: *"Behold, I come quickly: hold that fast which thou hast, that no man take thy crown"* (Revelation 3:11). Even the church in Philadelphia was in danger of losing its crown. This is not losing salvation, but it is missing God's best.

The grace of God is free even to the vilest sinner, but the thrones of the millennial age are won by sacrifice, service, and victorious achievement. The Lord is giving us opportunities continually to lose or win a crown. Let us give heed to the faithful admonition of the apostle of love to one of his cherished friends:

> Look to yourselves, that we lose not those things which we have wrought, but that we receive a full reward.   (2 John 1:8)

> And now, little children, abide in him; that, when he shall appear, we may have confidence, and not be ashamed before him at his coming.   (1 John 2:28)

ABOUT THE AUTHOR

Albert Benjamin Simpson (1843–1919) was born to parents of Scottish descent and grew to become one of the most respected Christian figures in American evangelicalism. A much-sought-after speaker and pastor, Simpson founded a major evangelical denomination, published more than seventy books, edited a weekly magazine for nearly forty years, and wrote many gospel songs and poems.

The first few years of his life were spent in relative simplicity on Prince Edward Island, Canada, where his father, an elder in the Presbyterian church, worked as a shipbuilder and eventually became involved in the export/import industry. To avoid an approaching business depression, the family moved to Ontario, where the younger Simpson accepted Christ as his Savior at age fifteen and was subsequently "called by God to preach" the gospel of Christ.

Simpson went on to pastor New York's 13th Street Presbyterian Church. However, in 1881, he resigned and began to hold independent evangelistic meetings in New York City. A year later, the Gospel Tabernacle was built, and Simpson began to turn his vision toward establishing an organization for missions. Simpson helped to form and lead two evangelization societies: The Christian Alliance and The Evangelical Missionary Alliance. As thousands joined these two groups, Simpson sensed a need for the two to become one. In 1897, they became The Christian and Missionary Alliance.

Welcome to Our House!

We Have a Special Gift for You ...

It is our privilege and pleasure to share in your love of Christian classics by publishing books that enrich your life and encourage your faith.

To show our appreciation, we invite you to sign up to receive a specially selected **Reader Appreciation Gift**, with our compliments. Just go to the Web address at the bottom of this page.

God bless you as you seek a deeper walk with Him!

WE HAVE A GIFT FOR YOU

whpub.me/classicthx

WHITAKER
HOUSE